TEACHER'S PET PUBLICATIONS

PUZZLE PACK
for
The Time Machine

based on the book by
H. G. Wells

Written by
Mary B. Collins

© 2008 Teacher's Pet Publications
All Rights Reserved

The materials in this packet are copyrighted
by Teacher's Pet Publications, Inc.

These pages may be duplicated by the purchaser
for use in the purchaser's own classroom.

Copying any of these materials and distributing them
for any other purpose is a violation of the copyright laws.

© 2008 Teacher's Pet Publications, Inc.
www.tpet.com

INTRODUCTION
If you already own the LitPlan for this title, this Puzzle Pack will refresh your Unit Resource Materials and Vocabulary Resource Materials sections plus give you additional materials you can substitute into the tests. If you do not already have a complete LitPlan, these pages will give you some supplemental materials to use with your own plan. There are two main groups of materials: one set for unit words (such as characters' names, symbols, places, etc.) and one set for vocabulary words associated with the book.

WORD LIST
There is a word list for both the unit words and the vocabulary words. These lists show you which words are being used in the materials and the clues or definitions being used for those words. You may want to give students a word list with clues/definitions to help them, or you may want students to only have a word list (without clues/definitions) if you want them to work a little harder. Both are available for duplication. The word lists can also be your "calling key" for the bingo games.

FILL IN THE BLANK AND MATCHING
There are 4 each of the fill in the blank and matching worksheets for both the unit and vocabulary words. These pages can be used either as extra worksheets for students or as objective parts of a unit test. They can be done individually if students need extra help or as a whole class activity to review the material covered.

MAGIC SQUARES
The magic squares not only reinforce the material covered but also work on reasoning and math skills. Many teachers have told us that their students really enjoy doing these!

WORD SEARCH PUZZLES
The word search words go in all directions, as indicated on your answer keys. Two of the word search puzzles have the clues listed rather than the words. This makes the puzzle a little more difficult, but it reinforces the material better. Two word search puzzles have words only for students who find the clue puzzles too difficult.

CROSSWORD PUZZLES
Both unit and vocabulary word sections have 4 crossword puzzles.

BINGO CARDS
There are 32 individual bingo cards for the unit words and 32 individual bingo cards for the vocabulary words. You can use your word list as a "call list," calling the words at random and marking them off of your list as you go, or you could use the flash cards by cutting them apart and drawing the words at random from a hat (or box or whatever). To make a better review, you might ask for the definition and spelling of each word as you call it out–or you could call out the definitions and have students tell you the words they need to look for on the puzzle.

JUGGLE LETTERS
The vocabulary juggle letter game is intended to help students learn the spellings of the words. One sheet has the definitions listed on it as an extra help for students who need it or to reinforce the definitions if you choose to do so.

FLASH CARDS
We've included a set of vocabulary flash cards you can duplicate, cut, and fold for your students. Some teachers make a few sets for general use by the class; others make a set for each student. Some teachers duplicate them for each student and have the students cut & fold their own. You can cut out just the words and put them in a hat, have each student pick out one word and write the definition and a sentence for that word. Students then swap words and papers, with the next student adding a sentence of his own under the last one. You can have students swap as many times as you like. Each time the student will read the sentences written prior to his own and then add a sentence. You can cut out the words and definitions separately and play "I Have; Who Has?" Each student in the room draws a word and definition. The first student says, "I have (the name of the word). Who has the definition?" The student with the definition reads it then says, "I have (the name of the vocabulary word she has). Who has the definition?" The round continues until all words and definitions have been given.

Time Machine Word List

No.	Word	Clue/Definition
1.	BLANK	Editor's name
2.	CAMPHOR	Volatile substance the Time Traveller found in the museum
3.	CHOSE	Silent Man's name
4.	CLOCK	Goes from 10:01 to 3:20 in just seconds
5.	CRAB	It attacked the Time Traveller in the far future; giant ___.
6.	DARKENSS	The Time Traveller dreaded this.
7.	DASH	Name of the Journalist
8.	DYNAMITE	Explosive the Time Traveller found in the museum
9.	EDITOR	He spoke first after the Traveller's tale.
10.	ELOI	They had a peaceful, fruit-eating society.
11.	FILBY	Argumentative person with red hair
12.	FIRE	Morlocks feared it.
13.	FLOWERS	Souvenir from the future; wilted ___
14.	FRUIT	Eloi survived on this food group.
15.	GAZETTE	Pall Mall ___ confirms the date the Time Traveller returns home.
16.	GROOVE	A clue as to where the time machine was hidden
17.	LEVERS	The Time Traveller kept these in his pocket.
18.	MACHINE	It was hidden inside the bronze pedestal.
19.	MATCHES	People of the future had not seen these.
20.	MEAT	Eloi were this to the Morlocks.
21.	MEDICAL	The ___ Man was instructed to begin dinner promptly at 7:00.
22.	MORLOCKS	Industrious, underground carnivores
23.	MUSEUM	The Palace of Green Porcelain
24.	NARRATOR	He kept the Time Traveller's souvenir from the future.
25.	OIL	Morlocks used this when cleaning the time machine.
26.	PLATO	The very young man wanted to hear Greek from ___'s lips.
27.	PSYCHOLOGIST	He presses the lever on the Time Machine model.
28.	RHODODENDRON	They surround the lawn where the Time Machine stops.
29.	RICHARDSON	Publisher the Time Traveller never got to meet with
30.	SALTPETER	The Time Traveller needs this to make gunpowder.
31.	SHOES	The Time Traveller threw these away when going through the forest with Weena.
32.	SILENT	The most nervous person in the room; the ___ Man
33.	SPHINX	Giant white statue in the forest
34.	STARS	They repositioned themselves over time.
35.	SUN	Eloi believed the Time Traveller came from this place.
36.	TIME	The fourth dimension
37.	TRAVELLER	He found himself on a very strange adventure; the Time ___
38.	UTOPIA	The Time Traveller compared the Eloi society to this.
39.	WATCHETT	Time Traveller's housekeeper
40.	WEENA	She nearly drowned.

Time Machine Fill In The Blank 1

_____
_____
_____
_____
_____
_____
_____
_____
_____
_____
_____
_____
_____
_____
_____
_____
_____
_____
_____
_____

1. The fourth dimension
2. The Time Traveller dreaded this.
3. People of the future had not seen these.
4. Morlocks feared it.
5. Pall Mall ___ confirms the date the Time Traveller returns home.
6. Volatile substance the Time Traveller found in the museum
7. Eloi survived on this food group.
8. Name of the Journalist
9. He found himself on a very strange adventure; the Time ___
10. Argumentative person with red hair
11. He spoke first after the Traveller's tale.
12. The Palace of Green Porcelain
13. The Time Traveller kept these in his pocket.
14. The Time Traveller threw these away when going through the forest with Weena.
15. Publisher the Time Traveller never got to meet with
16. The Time Traveller needs this to make gunpowder.
17. The very young man wanted to hear Greek from ___'s lips.
18. It was hidden inside the bronze pedestal.
19. The Time Traveller compared the Eloi society to this.
20. They surround the lawn where the Time Machine stops.

Time Machine Fill In The Blank 1 Answer Key

Answer	Clue
TIME	1. The fourth dimension
DARKENSS	2. The Time Traveller dreaded this.
MATCHES	3. People of the future had not seen these.
FIRE	4. Morlocks feared it.
GAZETTE	5. Pall Mall ___ confirms the date the Time Traveller returns home.
CAMPHOR	6. Volatile substance the Time Traveller found in the museum
FRUIT	7. Eloi survived on this food group.
DASH	8. Name of the Journalist
TRAVELLER	9. He found himself on a very strange adventure; the Time ___
FILBY	10. Argumentative person with red hair
EDITOR	11. He spoke first after the Traveller's tale.
MUSEUM	12. The Palace of Green Porcelain
LEVERS	13. The Time Traveller kept these in his pocket.
SHOES	14. The Time Traveller threw these away when going through the forest with Weena.
RICHARDSON	15. Publisher the Time Traveller never got to meet with
SALTPETER	16. The Time Traveller needs this to make gunpowder.
PLATO	17. The very young man wanted to hear Greek from ___'s lips.
MACHINE	18. It was hidden inside the bronze pedestal.
UTOPIA	19. The Time Traveller compared the Eloi society to this.
RHODODENDRON	20. They surround the lawn where the Time Machine stops.

Time Machine Fill In The Blank 2

1. He kept the Time Traveller's souvenir from the future.
2. The very young man wanted to hear Greek from ___'s lips.
3. The Time Traveller needs this to make gunpowder.
4. A clue as to where the time machine was hidden
5. It was hidden inside the bronze pedestal.
6. The Time Traveller threw these away when going through the forest with Weena.
7. He presses the lever on the Time Machine model.
8. Eloi believed the Time Traveller came from this place.
9. Eloi were this to the Morlocks.
10. They repositioned themselves over time.
11. Publisher the Time Traveller never got to meet with
12. The Time Traveller kept these in his pocket.
13. The most nervous person in the room; the ___ Man
14. Morlocks used this when cleaning the time machine.
15. Eloi survived on this food group.
16. Name of the Journalist
17. The fourth dimension
18. He spoke first after the Traveller's tale.
19. Goes from 10:01 to 3:20 in just seconds
20. The Time Traveller dreaded this.

Time Machine Fill In The Blank 2 Answer Key

NARRATOR	1. He kept the Time Traveller's souvenir from the future.
PLATO	2. The very young man wanted to hear Greek from ___'s lips.
SALTPETER	3. The Time Traveller needs this to make gunpowder.
GROOVE	4. A clue as to where the time machine was hidden
MACHINE	5. It was hidden inside the bronze pedestal.
SHOES	6. The Time Traveller threw these away when going through the forest with Weena.
PSYCHOLOGIST	7. He presses the lever on the Time Machine model.
SUN	8. Eloi believed the Time Traveller came from this place.
MEAT	9. Eloi were this to the Morlocks.
STARS	10. They repositioned themselves over time.
RICHARDSON	11. Publisher the Time Traveller never got to meet with
LEVERS	12. The Time Traveller kept these in his pocket.
SILENT	13. The most nervous person in the room; the ___ Man
OIL	14. Morlocks used this when cleaning the time machine.
FRUIT	15. Eloi survived on this food group.
DASH	16. Name of the Journalist
TIME	17. The fourth dimension
EDITOR	18. He spoke first after the Traveller's tale.
CLOCK	19. Goes from 10:01 to 3:20 in just seconds
DARKENSS	20. The Time Traveller dreaded this.

Time Machine Fill In The Blank 3

_____
_____
_____
_____
_____
_____
_____
_____
_____
_____
_____
_____
_____
_____
_____
_____
_____
_____
_____
_____

1. Souvenir from the future; wilted ___
2. The Time Traveller needs this to make gunpowder.
3. Morlocks used this when cleaning the time machine.
4. The Time Traveller kept these in his pocket.
5. It was hidden inside the bronze pedestal.
6. Pall Mall ___ confirms the date the Time Traveller returns home.
7. He spoke first after the Traveller's tale.
8. Publisher the Time Traveller never got to meet with
9. He kept the Time Traveller's souvenir from the future.
10. Morlocks feared it.
11. The Time Traveller compared the Eloi society to this.
12. It attacked the Time Traveller in the far future; giant ___.
13. The very young man wanted to hear Greek from ___'s lips.
14. Eloi survived on this food group.
15. They repositioned themselves over time.
16. The most nervous person in the room; the ___ Man
17. Time Traveller's housekeeper
18. Goes from 10:01 to 3:20 in just seconds
19. Volatile substance the Time Traveller found in the museum
20. She nearly drowned.

Time Machine Fill In The Blank 3 Answer Key

FLOWERS	1. Souvenir from the future; wilted ___
SALTPETER	2. The Time Traveller needs this to make gunpowder.
OIL	3. Morlocks used this when cleaning the time machine.
LEVERS	4. The Time Traveller kept these in his pocket.
MACHINE	5. It was hidden inside the bronze pedestal.
GAZETTE	6. Pall Mall ___ confirms the date the Time Traveller returns home.
EDITOR	7. He spoke first after the Traveller's tale.
RICHARDSON	8. Publisher the Time Traveller never got to meet with
NARRATOR	9. He kept the Time Traveller's souvenir from the future.
FIRE	10. Morlocks feared it.
UTOPIA	11. The Time Traveller compared the Eloi society to this.
CRAB	12. It attacked the Time Traveller in the far future; giant ___.
PLATO	13. The very young man wanted to hear Greek from ___'s lips.
FRUIT	14. Eloi survived on this food group.
STARS	15. They repositioned themselves over time.
SILENT	16. The most nervous person in the room; the ___ Man
WATCHETT	17. Time Traveller's housekeeper
CLOCK	18. Goes from 10:01 to 3:20 in just seconds
CAMPHOR	19. Volatile substance the Time Traveller found in the museum
WEENA	20. She nearly drowned.

Time Machine Fill In The Blank 4

1. They surround the lawn where the Time Machine stops.
2. Eloi were this to the Morlocks.
3. Eloi survived on this food group.
4. Explosive the Time Traveller found in the museum
5. Volatile substance the Time Traveller found in the museum
6. Giant white statue in the forest
7. The Time Traveller compared the Eloi society to this.
8. The most nervous person in the room; the ___ Man
9. He kept the Time Traveller's souvenir from the future.
10. Editor's name
11. Publisher the Time Traveller never got to meet with
12. Eloi believed the Time Traveller came from this place.
13. He found himself on a very strange adventure; the Time ___
14. The very young man wanted to hear Greek from ___'s lips.
15. Goes from 10:01 to 3:20 in just seconds
16. People of the future had not seen these.
17. Morlocks used this when cleaning the time machine.
18. The Palace of Green Porcelain
19. The Time Traveller dreaded this.
20. A clue as to where the time machine was hidden

Time Machine Fill In The Blank 4 Answer Key

Answer	#	Clue
RHODODENDRON	1.	They surround the lawn where the Time Machine stops.
MEAT	2.	Eloi were this to the Morlocks.
FRUIT	3.	Eloi survived on this food group.
DYNAMITE	4.	Explosive the Time Traveller found in the museum
CAMPHOR	5.	Volatile substance the Time Traveller found in the museum
SPHINX	6.	Giant white statue in the forest
UTOPIA	7.	The Time Traveller compared the Eloi society to this.
SILENT	8.	The most nervous person in the room; the ___ Man
NARRATOR	9.	He kept the Time Traveller's souvenir from the future.
BLANK	10.	Editor's name
RICHARDSON	11.	Publisher the Time Traveller never got to meet with
SUN	12.	Eloi believed the Time Traveller came from this place.
TRAVELLER	13.	He found himself on a very strange adventure; the Time ___
PLATO	14.	The very young man wanted to hear Greek from ___'s lips.
CLOCK	15.	Goes from 10:01 to 3:20 in just seconds
MATCHES	16.	People of the future had not seen these.
OIL	17.	Morlocks used this when cleaning the time machine.
MUSEUM	18.	The Palace of Green Porcelain
DARKENSS	19.	The Time Traveller dreaded this.
GROOVE	20.	A clue as to where the time machine was hidden

Time Machine Matching 1

___ 1. PLATO
___ 2. FRUIT
___ 3. RHODODENDRON
___ 4. CAMPHOR
___ 5. FLOWERS
___ 6. BLANK
___ 7. CLOCK
___ 8. SALTPETER
___ 9. RICHARDSON
___ 10. GROOVE
___ 11. UTOPIA
___ 12. STARS
___ 13. MUSEUM
___ 14. SUN
___ 15. CRAB
___ 16. PSYCHOLOGIST
___ 17. ELOI
___ 18. WEENA
___ 19. OIL
___ 20. MORLOCKS
___ 21. WATCHETT
___ 22. CHOSE
___ 23. SILENT
___ 24. SPHINX
___ 25. DASH

A. The most nervous person in the room; the ___ Man
B. The Time Traveller needs this to make gunpowder.
C. Volatile substance the Time Traveller found in the museum
D. He presses the lever on the Time Machine model.
E. Industrious, underground carnivores
F. Giant white statue in the forest
G. They repositioned themselves over time.
H. Publisher the Time Traveller never got to meet with
I. Silent Man's name
J. Name of the Journalist
K. They had a peaceful, fruit-eating society.
L. Editor's name
M. Time Traveller's housekeeper
N. It attacked the Time Traveller in the far future; giant ___.
O. The Palace of Green Porcelain
P. The very young man wanted to hear Greek from ___'s lips.
Q. Eloi survived on this food group.
R. A clue as to where the time machine was hidden
S. Eloi believed the Time Traveller came from this place.
T. She nearly drowned.
U. Goes from 10:01 to 3:20 in just seconds
V. The Time Traveller compared the Eloi society to this.
W. Souvenir from the future; wilted ___
X. Morlocks used this when cleaning the time machine.
Y. They surround the lawn where the Time Machine stops.

Time Machine Matching 1 Answer Key

P - 1. PLATO
Q - 2. FRUIT
Y - 3. RHODODENDRON
C - 4. CAMPHOR
W - 5. FLOWERS
L - 6. BLANK
U - 7. CLOCK
B - 8. SALTPETER
H - 9. RICHARDSON
R - 10. GROOVE
V - 11. UTOPIA
G - 12. STARS
O - 13. MUSEUM
S - 14. SUN
N - 15. CRAB
D - 16. PSYCHOLOGIST
K - 17. ELOI
T - 18. WEENA
X - 19. OIL
E - 20. MORLOCKS
M - 21. WATCHETT
I - 22. CHOSE
A - 23. SILENT
F - 24. SPHINX
J - 25. DASH

A. The most nervous person in the room; the ___ Man
B. The Time Traveller needs this to make gunpowder.
C. Volatile substance the Time Traveller found in the museum
D. He presses the lever on the Time Machine model.
E. Industrious, underground carnivores
F. Giant white statue in the forest
G. They repositioned themselves over time.
H. Publisher the Time Traveller never got to meet with
I. Silent Man's name
J. Name of the Journalist
K. They had a peaceful, fruit-eating society.
L. Editor's name
M. Time Traveller's housekeeper
N. It attacked the Time Traveller in the far future; giant ___.
O. The Palace of Green Porcelain
P. The very young man wanted to hear Greek from ___'s lips.
Q. Eloi survived on this food group.
R. A clue as to where the time machine was hidden
S. Eloi believed the Time Traveller came from this place.
T. She nearly drowned.
U. Goes from 10:01 to 3:20 in just seconds
V. The Time Traveller compared the Eloi society to this.
W. Souvenir from the future; wilted ___
X. Morlocks used this when cleaning the time machine.
Y. They surround the lawn where the Time Machine stops.

Time Machine Matching 2

___ 1. MATCHES
___ 2. RICHARDSON
___ 3. STARS
___ 4. CRAB
___ 5. WEENA
___ 6. FRUIT
___ 7. MORLOCKS
___ 8. FLOWERS
___ 9. MEAT
___ 10. FIRE
___ 11. DASH
___ 12. CLOCK
___ 13. UTOPIA
___ 14. LEVERS
___ 15. MACHINE
___ 16. TIME
___ 17. SUN
___ 18. SHOES
___ 19. DARKENSS
___ 20. OIL
___ 21. MEDICAL
___ 22. SPHINX
___ 23. EDITOR
___ 24. GROOVE
___ 25. NARRATOR

A. Publisher the Time Traveller never got to meet with
B. She nearly drowned.
C. He spoke first after the Traveller's tale.
D. The ___ Man was instructed to begin dinner promptly at 7:00.
E. It was hidden inside the bronze pedestal.
F. Morlocks used this when cleaning the time machine.
G. Eloi were this to the Morlocks.
H. The Time Traveller compared the Eloi society to this.
I. The Time Traveller threw these away when going through the forest with Weena.
J. People of the future had not seen these.
K. It attacked the Time Traveller in the far future; giant ___.
L. Name of the Journalist
M. Goes from 10:01 to 3:20 in just seconds
N. He kept the Time Traveller's souvenir from the future.
O. They repositioned themselves over time.
P. Eloi believed the Time Traveller came from this place.
Q. Industrious, underground carnivores
R. The Time Traveller kept these in his pocket.
S. The fourth dimension
T. Souvenir from the future; wilted ___
U. A clue as to where the time machine was hidden
V. Giant white statue in the forest
W. Eloi survived on this food group.
X. The Time Traveller dreaded this.
Y. Morlocks feared it.

Time Machine Matching 2 Answer Key

J - 1. MATCHES	A. Publisher the Time Traveller never got to meet with
A - 2. RICHARDSON	B. She nearly drowned.
O - 3. STARS	C. He spoke first after the Traveller's tale.
K - 4. CRAB	D. The ___ Man was instructed to begin dinner promptly at 7:00.
B - 5. WEENA	E. It was hidden inside the bronze pedestal.
W - 6. FRUIT	F. Morlocks used this when cleaning the time machine.
Q - 7. MORLOCKS	G. Eloi were this to the Morlocks.
T - 8. FLOWERS	H. The Time Traveller compared the Eloi society to this.
G - 9. MEAT	I. The Time Traveller threw these away when going through the forest with Weena.
Y - 10. FIRE	J. People of the future had not seen these.
L - 11. DASH	K. It attacked the Time Traveller in the far future; giant ___.
M - 12. CLOCK	L. Name of the Journalist
H - 13. UTOPIA	M. Goes from 10:01 to 3:20 in just seconds
R - 14. LEVERS	N. He kept the Time Traveller's souvenir from the future.
E - 15. MACHINE	O. They repositioned themselves over time.
S - 16. TIME	P. Eloi believed the Time Traveller came from this place.
P - 17. SUN	Q. Industrious, underground carnivores
I - 18. SHOES	R. The Time Traveller kept these in his pocket.
X - 19. DARKENSS	S. The fourth dimension
F - 20. OIL	T. Souvenir from the future; wilted ___
D - 21. MEDICAL	U. A clue as to where the time machine was hidden
V - 22. SPHINX	V. Giant white statue in the forest
C - 23. EDITOR	W. Eloi survived on this food group.
U - 24. GROOVE	X. The Time Traveller dreaded this.
N - 25. NARRATOR	Y. Morlocks feared it.

Time Machine Matching 3

___ 1. RICHARDSON
___ 2. SILENT
___ 3. TIME
___ 4. CAMPHOR
___ 5. SHOES
___ 6. SUN
___ 7. EDITOR
___ 8. GAZETTE
___ 9. FILBY
___ 10. MATCHES
___ 11. DASH
___ 12. FIRE
___ 13. CLOCK
___ 14. DYNAMITE
___ 15. MEAT
___ 16. NARRATOR
___ 17. MACHINE
___ 18. PSYCHOLOGIST
___ 19. FLOWERS
___ 20. GROOVE
___ 21. SPHINX
___ 22. TRAVELLER
___ 23. PLATO
___ 24. FRUIT
___ 25. MEDICAL

A. Pall Mall ___ confirms the date the Time Traveller returns home.
B. The ___ Man was instructed to begin dinner promptly at 7:00.
C. Eloi believed the Time Traveller came from this place.
D. Eloi survived on this food group.
E. The Time Traveller threw these away when going through the forest with Weena.
F. Argumentative person with red hair
G. He found himself on a very strange adventure; the Time ___
H. The very young man wanted to hear Greek from ___'s lips.
I. A clue as to where the time machine was hidden
J. He kept the Time Traveller's souvenir from the future.
K. The fourth dimension
L. Publisher the Time Traveller never got to meet with
M. The most nervous person in the room; the ___ Man
N. He spoke first after the Traveller's tale.
O. He presses the lever on the Time Machine model.
P. Explosive the Time Traveller found in the museum
Q. Name of the Journalist
R. It was hidden inside the bronze pedestal.
S. Volatile substance the Time Traveller found in the museum
T. Eloi were this to the Morlocks.
U. Souvenir from the future; wilted ___
V. People of the future had not seen these.
W. Giant white statue in the forest
X. Morlocks feared it.
Y. Goes from 10:01 to 3:20 in just seconds

Time Machine Matching 3 Answer Key

L - 1. RICHARDSON	A. Pall Mall ___ confirms the date the Time Traveller returns home.
M - 2. SILENT	B. The ___ Man was instructed to begin dinner promptly at 7:00.
K - 3. TIME	C. Eloi believed the Time Traveller came from this place.
S - 4. CAMPHOR	D. Eloi survived on this food group.
E - 5. SHOES	E. The Time Traveller threw these away when going through the forest with Weena.
C - 6. SUN	F. Argumentative person with red hair
N - 7. EDITOR	G. He found himself on a very strange adventure; the Time ___
A - 8. GAZETTE	H. The very young man wanted to hear Greek from ___'s lips.
F - 9. FILBY	I. A clue as to where the time machine was hidden
V - 10. MATCHES	J. He kept the Time Traveller's souvenir from the future.
Q - 11. DASH	K. The fourth dimension
X - 12. FIRE	L. Publisher the Time Traveller never got to meet with
Y - 13. CLOCK	M. The most nervous person in the room; the ___ Man
P - 14. DYNAMITE	N. He spoke first after the Traveller's tale.
T - 15. MEAT	O. He presses the lever on the Time Machine model.
J - 16. NARRATOR	P. Explosive the Time Traveller found in the museum
R - 17. MACHINE	Q. Name of the Journalist
O - 18. PSYCHOLOGIST	R. It was hidden inside the bronze pedestal.
U - 19. FLOWERS	S. Volatile substance the Time Traveller found in the museum
I - 20. GROOVE	T. Eloi were this to the Morlocks.
W - 21. SPHINX	U. Souvenir from the future; wilted ___
G - 22. TRAVELLER	V. People of the future had not seen these.
H - 23. PLATO	W. Giant white statue in the forest
D - 24. FRUIT	X. Morlocks feared it.
B - 25. MEDICAL	Y. Goes from 10:01 to 3:20 in just seconds

Time Machine Matching 4

___ 1. SPHINX
___ 2. WATCHETT
___ 3. FLOWERS
___ 4. WEENA
___ 5. FRUIT
___ 6. RICHARDSON
___ 7. DASH
___ 8. CLOCK
___ 9. GROOVE
___10. GAZETTE
___11. CHOSE
___12. OIL
___13. DYNAMITE
___14. SUN
___15. BLANK
___16. TRAVELLER
___17. PLATO
___18. SHOES
___19. UTOPIA
___20. RHODODENDRON
___21. MORLOCKS
___22. FILBY
___23. PSYCHOLOGIST
___24. CAMPHOR
___25. SILENT

A. Silent Man's name
B. Souvenir from the future; wilted ___
C. He found himself on a very strange adventure; the Time ___
D. He presses the lever on the Time Machine model.
E. Eloi believed the Time Traveller came from this place.
F. Eloi survived on this food group.
G. The very young man wanted to hear Greek from ___'s lips.
H. Time Traveller's housekeeper
I. Morlocks used this when cleaning the time machine.
J. A clue as to where the time machine was hidden
K. They surround the lawn where the Time Machine stops.
L. The most nervous person in the room; the ___ Man
M. Pall Mall ___ confirms the date the Time Traveller returns home.
N. Industrious, underground carnivores
O. Publisher the Time Traveller never got to meet with
P. The Time Traveller threw these away when going through the forest with Weena.
Q. Editor's name
R. The Time Traveller compared the Eloi society to this.
S. Explosive the Time Traveller found in the museum
T. She nearly drowned.
U. Argumentative person with red hair
V. Name of the Journalist
W. Goes from 10:01 to 3:20 in just seconds
X. Giant white statue in the forest
Y. Volatile substance the Time Traveller found in the museum

Time Machine Matching 4 Answer Key

X - 1. SPHINX
H - 2. WATCHETT
B - 3. FLOWERS
T - 4. WEENA
F - 5. FRUIT
O - 6. RICHARDSON
V - 7. DASH
W - 8. CLOCK
J - 9. GROOVE
M -10. GAZETTE
A -11. CHOSE
I - 12. OIL
S -13. DYNAMITE
E -14. SUN
Q -15. BLANK
C -16. TRAVELLER
G -17. PLATO
P -18. SHOES
R -19. UTOPIA
K -20. RHODODENDRON
N -21. MORLOCKS
U -22. FILBY
D -23. PSYCHOLOGIST
Y -24. CAMPHOR
L -25. SILENT

A. Silent Man's name
B. Souvenir from the future; wilted ___
C. He found himself on a very strange adventure; the Time ___
D. He presses the lever on the Time Machine model.
E. Eloi believed the Time Traveller came from this place.
F. Eloi survived on this food group.
G. The very young man wanted to hear Greek from ___'s lips.
H. Time Traveller's housekeeper
I. Morlocks used this when cleaning the time machine.
J. A clue as to where the time machine was hidden
K. They surround the lawn where the Time Machine stops.
L. The most nervous person in the room; the ___ Man
M. Pall Mall ___ confirms the date the Time Traveller returns home.
N. Industrious, underground carnivores
O. Publisher the Time Traveller never got to meet with
P. The Time Traveller threw these away when going through the forest with Weena.
Q. Editor's name
R. The Time Traveller compared the Eloi society to this.
S. Explosive the Time Traveller found in the museum
T. She nearly drowned.
U. Argumentative person with red hair
V. Name of the Journalist
W. Goes from 10:01 to 3:20 in just seconds
X. Giant white statue in the forest
Y. Volatile substance the Time Traveller found in the museum

Time Machine Magic Squares 1

Match the definition with the vocabulary word. Put your answers in the magic squares below. When your answers are correct, all columns and rows will add to the same number.

A. STARS
B. MACHINE
C. FRUIT
D. DARKENSS
E. FIRE
F. UTOPIA
G. PSYCHOLOGIST
H. TIME
I. BLANK
J. SALTPETER
K. CHOSE
L. SPHINX
M. TRAVELLER
N. MUSEUM
O. RHODODENDRON
P. SHOES

1. Eloi survived on this food group.
2. The Time Traveller needs this to make gunpowder.
3. The Time Traveller compared the Eloi society to this.
4. They surround the lawn where the Time Machine stops.
5. The Time Traveller threw these away when going through the forest with Weena.
6. Morlocks feared it.
7. Editor's name
8. The Time Traveller dreaded this.
9. He found himself on a very strange adventure; the Time ___
10. The fourth dimension
11. Giant white statue in the forest
12. They repositioned themselves over time.
13. It was hidden inside the bronze pedestal.
14. Silent Man's name
15. He presses the lever on the Time Machine model.
16. The Palace of Green Porcelain

A=	B=	C=	D=
E=	F=	G=	H=
I=	J=	K=	L=
M=	N=	O=	P=

Time Machine Magic Squares 1 Answer Key

Match the definition with the vocabulary word. Put your answers in the magic squares below. When your answers are correct, all columns and rows will add to the same number.

A. STARS
B. MACHINE
C. FRUIT
D. DARKENSS
E. FIRE
F. UTOPIA
G. PSYCHOLOGIST
H. TIME
I. BLANK
J. SALTPETER
K. CHOSE
L. SPHINX
M. TRAVELLER
N. MUSEUM
O. RHODODENDRON
P. SHOES

1. Eloi survived on this food group.
2. The Time Traveller needs this to make gunpowder.
3. The Time Traveller compared the Eloi society to this.
4. They surround the lawn where the Time Machine stops.
5. The Time Traveller threw these away when going through the forest with Weena.
6. Morlocks feared it.
7. Editor's name
8. The Time Traveller dreaded this.
9. He found himself on a very strange adventure; the Time ___
10. The fourth dimension
11. Giant white statue in the forest
12. They repositioned themselves over time.
13. It was hidden inside the bronze pedestal.
14. Silent Man's name
15. He presses the lever on the Time Machine model.
16. The Palace of Green Porcelain

A=12	B=13	C=1	D=8
E=6	F=3	G=15	H=10
I=7	J=2	K=14	L=11
M=9	N=16	O=4	P=5

Time Machine Magic Squares 2

Match the definition with the vocabulary word. Put your answers in the magic squares below. When your answers are correct, all columns and rows will add to the same number.

A. TIME
B. SHOES
C. MEDICAL
D. GAZETTE
E. PSYCHOLOGIST
F. SALTPETER
G. MEAT
H. OIL
I. WEENA
J. CHOSE
K. SILENT
L. CRAB
M. BLANK
N. RICHARDSON
O. MORLOCKS
P. DASH

1. The Time Traveller needs this to make gunpowder.
2. She nearly drowned.
3. Industrious, underground carnivores
4. Pall Mall ___ confirms the date the Time Traveller returns home.
5. Editor's name
6. The Time Traveller threw these away when going through the forest with Weena.
7. Morlocks used this when cleaning the time machine.
8. The most nervous person in the room; the ___ Man
9. The ___ Man was instructed to begin dinner promptly at 7:00.
10. Name of the Journalist
11. Silent Man's name
12. He presses the lever on the Time Machine model.
13. It attacked the Time Traveller in the far future; giant ___.
14. Eloi were this to the Morlocks.
15. The fourth dimension
16. Publisher the Time Traveller never got to meet with

A=	B=	C=	D=
E=	F=	G=	H=
I=	J=	K=	L=
M=	N=	O=	P=

23
Copyrighted

Time Machine Magic Squares 2 Answer Key

Match the definition with the vocabulary word. Put your answers in the magic squares below. When your answers are correct, all columns and rows will add to the same number.

A. TIME
B. SHOES
C. MEDICAL
D. GAZETTE
E. PSYCHOLOGIST
F. SALTPETER
G. MEAT
H. OIL
I. WEENA
J. CHOSE
K. SILENT
L. CRAB
M. BLANK
N. RICHARDSON
O. MORLOCKS
P. DASH

1. The Time Traveller needs this to make gunpowder.
2. She nearly drowned.
3. Industrious, underground carnivores
4. Pall Mall ___ confirms the date the Time Traveller returns home.
5. Editor's name
6. The Time Traveller threw these away when going through the forest with Weena.
7. Morlocks used this when cleaning the time machine.
8. The most nervous person in the room; the ___ Man
9. The ___ Man was instructed to begin dinner promptly at 7:00.
10. Name of the Journalist
11. Silent Man's name
12. He presses the lever on the Time Machine model.
13. It attacked the Time Traveller in the far future; giant ___.
14. Eloi were this to the Morlocks.
15. The fourth dimension
16. Publisher the Time Traveller never got to meet with

A=15	B=6	C=9	D=4
E=12	F=1	G=14	H=7
I=2	J=11	K=8	L=13
M=5	N=16	O=3	P=10

Time Machine Magic Squares 3

Match the definition with the vocabulary word. Put your answers in the magic squares below. When your answers are correct, all columns and rows will add to the same number.

A. MEDICAL
B. MEAT
C. MACHINE
D. SPHINX
E. NARRATOR
F. LEVERS
G. SALTPETER
H. TRAVELLER
I. ELOI
J. GROOVE
K. MUSEUM
L. DYNAMITE
M. BLANK
N. PLATO
O. FILBY
P. GAZETTE

1. The ___ Man was instructed to begin dinner promptly at 7:00.
2. The very young man wanted to hear Greek from ___'s lips.
3. A clue as to where the time machine was hidden
4. He kept the Time Traveller's souvenir from the future.
5. The Time Traveller needs this to make gunpowder.
6. Explosive the Time Traveller found in the museum
7. Pall Mall ___ confirms the date the Time Traveller returns home.
8. It was hidden inside the bronze pedestal.
9. Argumentative person with red hair
10. Giant white statue in the forest
11. He found himself on a very strange adventure; the Time ___
12. The Palace of Green Porcelain
13. They had a peaceful, fruit-eating society.
14. The Time Traveller kept these in his pocket.
15. Eloi were this to the Morlocks.
16. Editor's name

A=	B=	C=	D=
E=	F=	G=	H=
I=	J=	K=	L=
M=	N=	O=	P=

Time Machine Magic Squares 3 Answer Key

Match the definition with the vocabulary word. Put your answers in the magic squares below. When your answers are correct, all columns and rows will add to the same number.

A. MEDICAL
B. MEAT
C. MACHINE
D. SPHINX
E. NARRATOR
F. LEVERS
G. SALTPETER
H. TRAVELLER
I. ELOI
J. GROOVE
K. MUSEUM
L. DYNAMITE
M. BLANK
N. PLATO
O. FILBY
P. GAZETTE

1. The ___ Man was instructed to begin dinner promptly at 7:00.
2. The very young man wanted to hear Greek from ___'s lips.
3. A clue as to where the time machine was hidden
4. He kept the Time Traveller's souvenir from the future.
5. The Time Traveller needs this to make gunpowder.
6. Explosive the Time Traveller found in the museum
7. Pall Mall ___ confirms the date the Time Traveller returns home.
8. It was hidden inside the bronze pedestal.
9. Argumentative person with red hair
10. Giant white statue in the forest
11. He found himself on a very strange adventure; the Time ___
12. The Palace of Green Porcelain
13. They had a peaceful, fruit-eating society.
14. The Time Traveller kept these in his pocket.
15. Eloi were this to the Morlocks.
16. Editor's name

A=1	B=15	C=8	D=10
E=4	F=14	G=5	H=11
I=13	J=3	K=12	L=6
M=16	N=2	O=9	P=7

Time Machine Magic Squares 4

Match the definition with the vocabulary word. Put your answers in the magic squares below. When your answers are correct, all columns and rows will add to the same number.

A. BLANK
B. WATCHETT
C. MATCHES
D. MACHINE
E. CAMPHOR
F. FLOWERS
G. EDITOR
H. RHODODENDRON
I. SILENT
J. FRUIT
K. CHOSE
L. STARS
M. TIME
N. DARKENSS
O. MEAT
P. SUN

1. They surround the lawn where the Time Machine stops.
2. The fourth dimension
3. Time Traveller's housekeeper
4. Silent Man's name
5. Eloi survived on this food group.
6. People of the future had not seen these.
7. Eloi believed the Time Traveller came from this place.
8. Volatile substance the Time Traveller found in the museum
9. Eloi were this to the Morlocks.
10. Souvenir from the future; wilted ___
11. The most nervous person in the room; the ___ Man
12. It was hidden inside the bronze pedestal.
13. Editor's name
14. They repositioned themselves over time.
15. He spoke first after the Traveller's tale.
16. The Time Traveller dreaded this.

A=	B=	C=	D=
E=	F=	G=	H=
I=	J=	K=	L=
M=	N=	O=	P=

Time Machine Magic Squares 4 Answer Key

Match the definition with the vocabulary word. Put your answers in the magic squares below. When your answers are correct, all columns and rows will add to the same number.

A. BLANK
B. WATCHETT
C. MATCHES
D. MACHINE
E. CAMPHOR
F. FLOWERS
G. EDITOR
H. RHODODENDRON
I. SILENT
J. FRUIT
K. CHOSE
L. STARS
M. TIME
N. DARKENSS
O. MEAT
P. SUN

1. They surround the lawn where the Time Machine stops.
2. The fourth dimension
3. Time Traveller's housekeeper
4. Silent Man's name
5. Eloi survived on this food group.
6. People of the future had not seen these.
7. Eloi believed the Time Traveller came from this place.
8. Volatile substance the Time Traveller found in the museum
9. Eloi were this to the Morlocks.
10. Souvenir from the future; wilted ___
11. The most nervous person in the room; the ___ Man
12. It was hidden inside the bronze pedestal.
13. Editor's name
14. They repositioned themselves over time.
15. He spoke first after the Traveller's tale.
16. The Time Traveller dreaded this.

A=13	B=3	C=6	D=12
E=8	F=10	G=15	H=1
I=11	J=5	K=4	L=14
M=2	N=16	O=9	P=7

Time Machine Word Search 1

```
G E L O I T K F I R E C T T M C S W
A N P T C N S Y S O H M P A B A T X
Z N D A A D R H Z T S A T F P M A D
E W M L W E N A I Y C M I S P R K
T R B P K W W F H D H E L Y H S H
T S U M Q S O R Q E N I D B C O D N
E D T C U D L U S P A N I Y H R Q J
V A O L S S F I W R R E C G O V R Q
G R P O P X E T X E R T A N L X S G
R K I C Y S V U T F A C L L O Y P T
O E A K E K V E M S T D H S G S H F
O N R O N N P H R F O A S O I K I F
V S H Y Y T C E P T R S D L S P N B
E S U N L R V W A T C H E T T E X W
P N X A K E C E H D Y N A M I T E K
H L S M L H M E M I T C R A B O I L
```

A clue as to where the time machine was hidden (6)
Argumentative person with red hair (5)
Editor's name (5)
Eloi believed the Time Traveller came from this place. (3)
Eloi survived on this food group. (5)
Eloi were this to the Morlocks. (4)
Explosive the Time Traveller found in the museum (8)
Giant white statue in the forest (6)
Goes from 10:01 to 3:20 in just seconds (5)
He kept the Time Traveller's souvenir from the future. (8)
He presses the lever on the Time Machine model. (12)
He spoke first after the Traveller's tale. (6)
It attacked the Time Traveller in the far future; giant ___. (4)
It was hidden inside the bronze pedestal. (7)
Morlocks feared it. (4)
Morlocks used this when cleaning the time machine. (3)
Name of the Journalist (4)
Pall Mall ___ confirms the date the Time Traveller returns home. (7)
People of the future had not seen these. (7)
She nearly drowned. (5)
Silent Man's name (5)
Souvenir from the future; wilted ___ (7)
The Palace of Green Porcelain (6)
The Time Traveller compared the Eloi society to this. (6)
The Time Traveller dreaded this. (8)
The Time Traveller kept these in his pocket. (6)
The Time Traveller needs this to make gunpowder. (9)
The Time Traveller threw these away when going through the forest with Weena. (5)
The ___ Man was instructed to begin dinner promptly at 7:00. (7)
The fourth dimension (4)
The most nervous person in the room; the ___ Man (6)
The very young man wanted to hear Greek from ___'s lips. (5)
They had a peaceful, fruit-eating society. (4)
They repositioned themselves over time. (5)
Time Traveller's housekeeper (8)
Volatile substance the Time Traveller found in the museum (7)

Time Machine Word Search 1 Answer Key

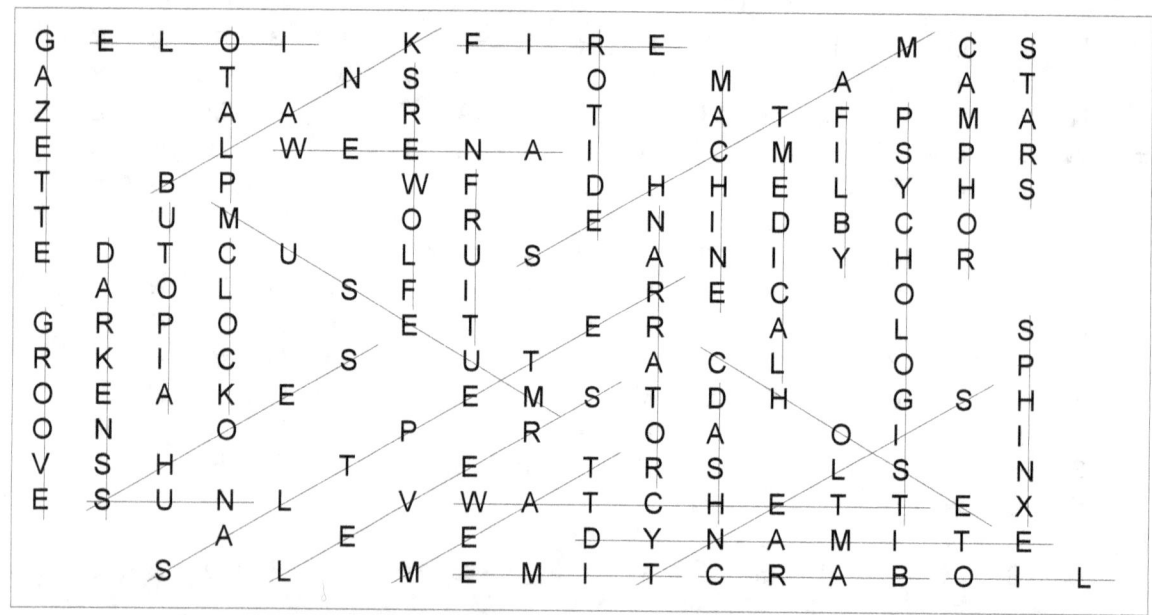

A clue as to where the time machine was hidden (6)
Argumentative person with red hair (5)
Editor's name (5)
Eloi believed the Time Traveller came from this place. (3)
Eloi survived on this food group. (5)
Eloi were this to the Morlocks. (4)
Explosive the Time Traveller found in the museum (8)
Giant white statue in the forest (6)
Goes from 10:01 to 3:20 in just seconds (5)
He kept the Time Traveller's souvenir from the future. (8)
He presses the lever on the Time Machine model. (12)
He spoke first after the Traveller's tale. (6)
It attacked the Time Traveller in the far future; giant ___. (4)
It was hidden inside the bronze pedestal. (7)
Morlocks feared it. (4)
Morlocks used this when cleaning the time machine. (3)
Name of the Journalist (4)
Pall Mall ___ confirms the date the Time Traveller returns home. (7)
People of the future had not seen these. (7)

She nearly drowned. (5)
Silent Man's name (5)
Souvenir from the future; wilted ___ (7)
The Palace of Green Porcelain (6)
The Time Traveller compared the Eloi society to this. (6)
The Time Traveller dreaded this. (8)
The Time Traveller kept these in his pocket. (6)
The Time Traveller needs this to make gunpowder. (9)
The Time Traveller threw these away when going through the forest with Weena. (5)
The ___ Man was instructed to begin dinner promptly at 7:00. (7)
The fourth dimension (4)
The most nervous person in the room; the ___ Man (6)
The very young man wanted to hear Greek from ___'s lips. (5)
They had a peaceful, fruit-eating society. (4)
They repositioned themselves over time. (5)
Time Traveller's housekeeper (8)
Volatile substance the Time Traveller found in the museum (7)

Time Machine Word Search 2

S	T	A	R	S	W	M	U	X	N	R	S	R	E	W	O	L	F
D	D	M	U	Y	B	U	T	R	P	H	R	M	L	L	R	B	M
B	P	N	W	M	Y	S	O	C	H	O	W	H	O	R	O	C	S
T	L	M	E	V	X	E	P	V	Y	D	R	X	I	Y	M	I	E
R	G	A	E	F	R	U	I	T	R	O	T	A	L	P	X	R	S
A	A	T	N	J	G	M	A	E	T	D	G	S	M	M	I	O	V
V	Z	C	A	K	W	L	T	A	K	E	R	G	X	F	J	H	M
E	E	H	F	T	K	E	R	C	T	N	O	X	N	I	H	P	S
L	T	E	B	H	P	R	Y	N	M	D	O	H	F	Y	E	M	W
L	T	S	F	T	A	B	E	O	W	R	V	K	M	N	T	A	D
E	E	C	L	N	L	L	R	Y	R	O	E	E	I	G	T	C	Z
R	C	A	P	I	I	L	T	O	T	N	D	H	Z	C	S	H	D
P	S	L	F	S	O	C	T	M	Y	I	C	B	H	H	X	O	Y
B	X	L	O	C	D	I	R	E	C	A	S	E	O	V	S	S	J
W	N	Z	K	C	D	Y	N	A	M	I	T	E	M	I	T	E	B
D	A	S	H	E	K	X	L	T	B	T	S	R	E	V	E	L	K

A clue as to where the time machine was hidden (6)
Argumentative person with red hair (5)
Editor's name (5)
Eloi believed the Time Traveller came from this place. (3)
Eloi survived on this food group. (5)
Eloi were this to the Morlocks. (4)
Explosive the Time Traveller found in the museum (8)
Giant white statue in the forest (6)
Goes from 10:01 to 3:20 in just seconds (5)
He found himself on a very strange adventure; the Time ___ (9)
He kept the Time Traveller's souvenir from the future. (8)
He spoke first after the Traveller's tale. (6)
Industrious, underground carnivores (8)
It attacked the Time Traveller in the far future; giant ___. (4)
It was hidden inside the bronze pedestal. (7)
Morlocks feared it. (4)
Morlocks used this when cleaning the time machine. (3)
Name of the Journalist (4)
Pall Mall ___ confirms the date the Time Traveller returns home. (7)
People of the future had not seen these. (7)
She nearly drowned. (5)
Silent Man's name (5)
Souvenir from the future; wilted ___ (7)
The Palace of Green Porcelain (6)
The Time Traveller compared the Eloi society to this. (6)
The Time Traveller kept these in his pocket. (6)
The Time Traveller needs this to make gunpowder. (9)
The Time Traveller threw these away when going through the forest with Weena. (5)
The ___ Man was instructed to begin dinner promptly at 7:00. (7)
The fourth dimension (4)
The most nervous person in the room; the ___ Man (6)
The very young man wanted to hear Greek from ___'s lips. (5)
They had a peaceful, fruit-eating society. (4)
They repositioned themselves over time. (5)
They surround the lawn where the Time Machine stops. (12)
Time Traveller's housekeeper (8)
Volatile substance the Time Traveller found in the museum (7)

Time Machine Word Search 2 Answer Key

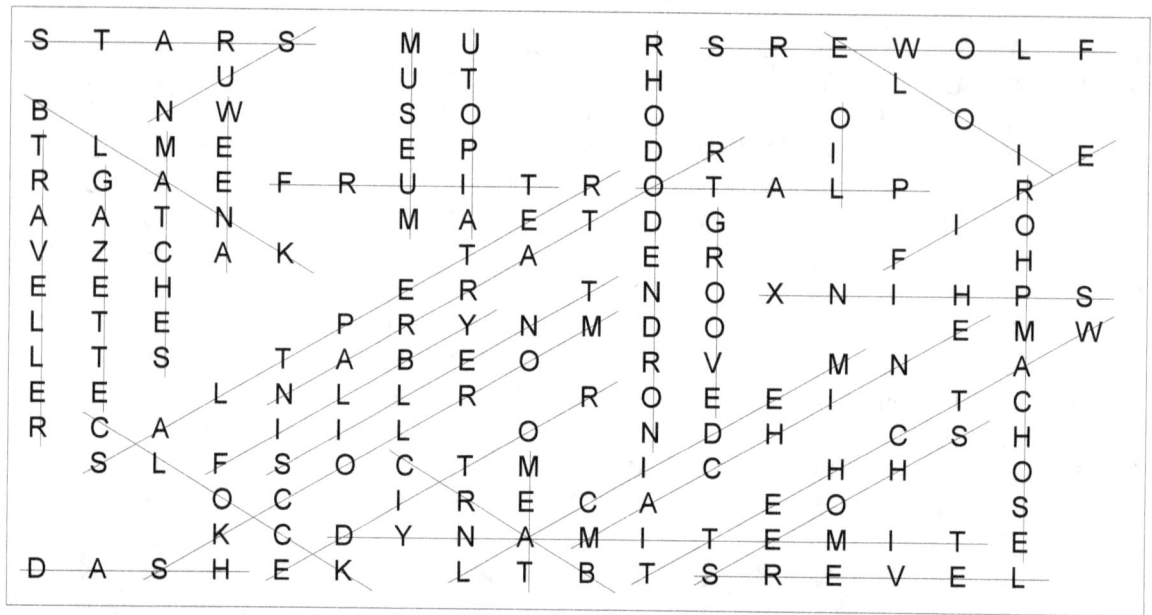

- A clue as to where the time machine was hidden (6)
- Argumentative person with red hair (5)
- Editor's name (5)
- Eloi believed the Time Traveller came from this place. (3)
- Eloi survived on this food group. (5)
- Eloi were this to the Morlocks. (4)
- Explosive the Time Traveller found in the museum (8)
- Giant white statue in the forest (6)
- Goes from 10:01 to 3:20 in just seconds (5)
- He found himself on a very strange adventure; the Time ___ (9)
- He kept the Time Traveller's souvenir from the future. (8)
- He spoke first after the Traveller's tale. (6)
- Industrious, underground carnivores (8)
- It attacked the Time Traveller in the far future; giant ___. (4)
- It was hidden inside the bronze pedestal. (7)
- Morlocks feared it. (4)
- Morlocks used this when cleaning the time machine. (3)
- Name of the Journalist (4)
- Pall Mall ___ confirms the date the Time Traveller returns home. (7)
- People of the future had not seen these. (7)
- She nearly drowned. (5)
- Silent Man's name (5)
- Souvenir from the future; wilted ___ (7)
- The Palace of Green Porcelain (6)
- The Time Traveller compared the Eloi society to this. (6)
- The Time Traveller kept these in his pocket. (6)
- The Time Traveller needs this to make gunpowder. (9)
- The Time Traveller threw these away when going through the forest with Weena. (5)
- The ___ Man was instructed to begin dinner promptly at 7:00. (7)
- The fourth dimension (4)
- The most nervous person in the room; the ___ Man (6)
- The very young man wanted to hear Greek from ___'s lips. (5)
- They had a peaceful, fruit-eating society. (4)
- They repositioned themselves over time. (5)
- They surround the lawn where the Time Machine stops. (12)
- Time Traveller's housekeeper (8)
- Volatile substance the Time Traveller found in the museum (7)

Time Machine Word Seach 3

```
M E A T F S B Z F R U I T C S M Q D C N
U V M U N I A C M L R N R H G H C T G R
S O O T T R L L Z C O W A O T H O A P P
E O R S E O R B T S F W V S W K Z E Q B
U R L K D T P T Y P Y Y E E L E F G S Y
M G O W I A S I D T E L R T J T W G W
W T C J T R B D A S M T L T S C L W D N
Y K K T O R J C L I L Q E T E S M H O N
L V S V R A R R Q G C D R R T D E S Z T
X Z L F C N K N M O B R Q P I Y D J K B
R D S Z A S C T V L T S M W M R I J L W
X E A P M S T S G O P L A G A L C W S Z
V N J S P E T N F H M I T H N E A I W Q
T I Z M H B N A I C L O C K Y V L Q E N
D H N C O E L N R Y F I H P D E P L E X
N C T H R L X A E S R H E J N R P M N C
T A K G V O B K N P N U S T X S I S A P
W M T V J I D A R K E N S S O T A L P N
```

BLANK	FRUIT	PSYCHOLOGIST
CAMPHOR	GAZETTE	RICHARDSON
CHOSE	GROOVE	SALTPETER
CLOCK	LEVERS	SHOES
CRAB	MACHINE	SILENT
DARKENSS	MATCHES	SPHINX
DASH	MEAT	STARS
DYNAMITE	MEDICAL	SUN
EDITOR	MORLOCKS	TIME
ELOI	MUSEUM	TRAVELLER
FILBY	NARRATOR	UTOPIA
FIRE	OIL	WATCHETT
FLOWERS	PLATO	WEENA

Time Machine Word Seach 3 Answer Key

```
M E A T F S         F R U I T   C   S
U   V   M U   A     L     T     H       H       G
S   O   O R   L     O     R     O       O   A   A
E   O   R L   B     W     A     S       Z   E   S
U   R   L O   Y     E     V     E       E
M   G   O C   P     L     E     R           M       N
            K T   I A     L     T           E       O
              E R   S     E     S           D
              D A   I     R     E           I
              I N   G           T           C
              T     O           I           A
D       T     O     L     S M   M       R   L
E   A   S S   R     O     P A   A       L       S
N       P E   C     G     L T   N       E       W
I   S   H B   A     Y     I C   Y       V       E
H       O E   M         F C H       K   D       E
C       R L   P     T   I L E           N       N
A           O R     A   R O S       T       M   A
W M         I       L   E C K       S   I       P
            D A R K E N S S     O       T L
```

BLANK
CAMPHOR
CHOSE
CLOCK
CRAB
DARKENSS
DASH
DYNAMITE
EDITOR
ELOI
FILBY
FIRE
FLOWERS

FRUIT
GAZETTE
GROOVE
LEVERS
MACHINE
MATCHES
MEAT
MEDICAL
MORLOCKS
MUSEUM
NARRATOR
OIL
PLATO

PSYCHOLOGIST
RICHARDSON
SALTPETER
SHOES
SILENT
SPHINX
STARS
SUN
TIME
TRAVELLER
UTOPIA
WATCHETT
WEENA

Time Machine Word Seach 4

```
C R I C H A R D S O N M Q W D T Y T Y S
H J L L H T J S T D T H S T Y I I M H G
O B Y O C X Q S R G S E R M B U E M M H
S E H C T A M O R L O C K S L R L N E P
E P R K J X H V E H O P N M I F O N D W
W A H T E P S V S B S I A F F S I G I V
B E A I M D E K N E A R L Q R H S R C H
Z E E A N R I U T H L H B C C C I O A G
M T C N S X S T C D T O N A T L L O L F
U I Y N A F E S O T P D M Z F R E V H Q
S M F L B Z S S T R E O T A L P N E H V
E A D Y A H R T X A T D Q I O Z T S J B
U N R G F A E M Z V E E J P W H A K C J
M Y V D T H L R P E R N G O E D H K M V
C D X S C S F X W L W D L T R X C V T K
H D J T P G J H Y L J R N U S X T X Y D
R V A M Z S C L P E K O K B R H L Y B N
N W N A R R A T O R Q N D A R K E N S S
```

BLANK

CAMPHOR

CHOSE

CLOCK

CRAB

DARKENSS

DASH

DYNAMITE

EDITOR

ELOI

FILBY

FIRE

FLOWERS

FRUIT

GAZETTE

GROOVE

LEVERS

MACHINE

MATCHES

MEAT

MEDICAL

MORLOCKS

MUSEUM

NARRATOR

OIL

PLATO

RHODODENDRON

RICHARDSON

SALTPETER

SHOES

SILENT

SPHINX

STARS

SUN

TIME

TRAVELLER

UTOPIA

WATCHETT

WEENA

Time Machine Word Seach 4 Answer Key

```
C R I C H A R D S O N                    T
H   L                       S     Y  I   I
O   O                       E     B  E   M
S E H C T A M O R L O C K S L  T  L  L   M  M
E P R     H   R   O   N    I  U  I  O    E
W A H   P V   E   S   A    F  R  F  I    D
B E A E  D E  S  I   L    F  H  C  S    I
E E T M  R N  T  R   B       A  F  L    C
M T C N  X S  E  H   M       L  L  E    A
U I       E   T  O           P  O  N    L
S M      Z     R  D           L  W  T
E A      A     A  O           O  E  A
U N      G    T   D           W  R
M Y      S    H   E           E  S
  D           A   R
              T
W N A R R A T O R       D A R K E N S S
```

BLANK	FRUIT	RHODODENDRON
CAMPHOR	GAZETTE	RICHARDSON
CHOSE	GROOVE	SALTPETER
CLOCK	LEVERS	SHOES
CRAB	MACHINE	SILENT
DARKENSS	MATCHES	SPHINX
DASH	MEAT	STARS
DYNAMITE	MEDICAL	SUN
EDITOR	MORLOCKS	TIME
ELOI	MUSEUM	TRAVELLER
FILBY	NARRATOR	UTOPIA
FIRE	OIL	WATCHETT
FLOWERS	PLATO	WEENA

Time Machine Crossword 1

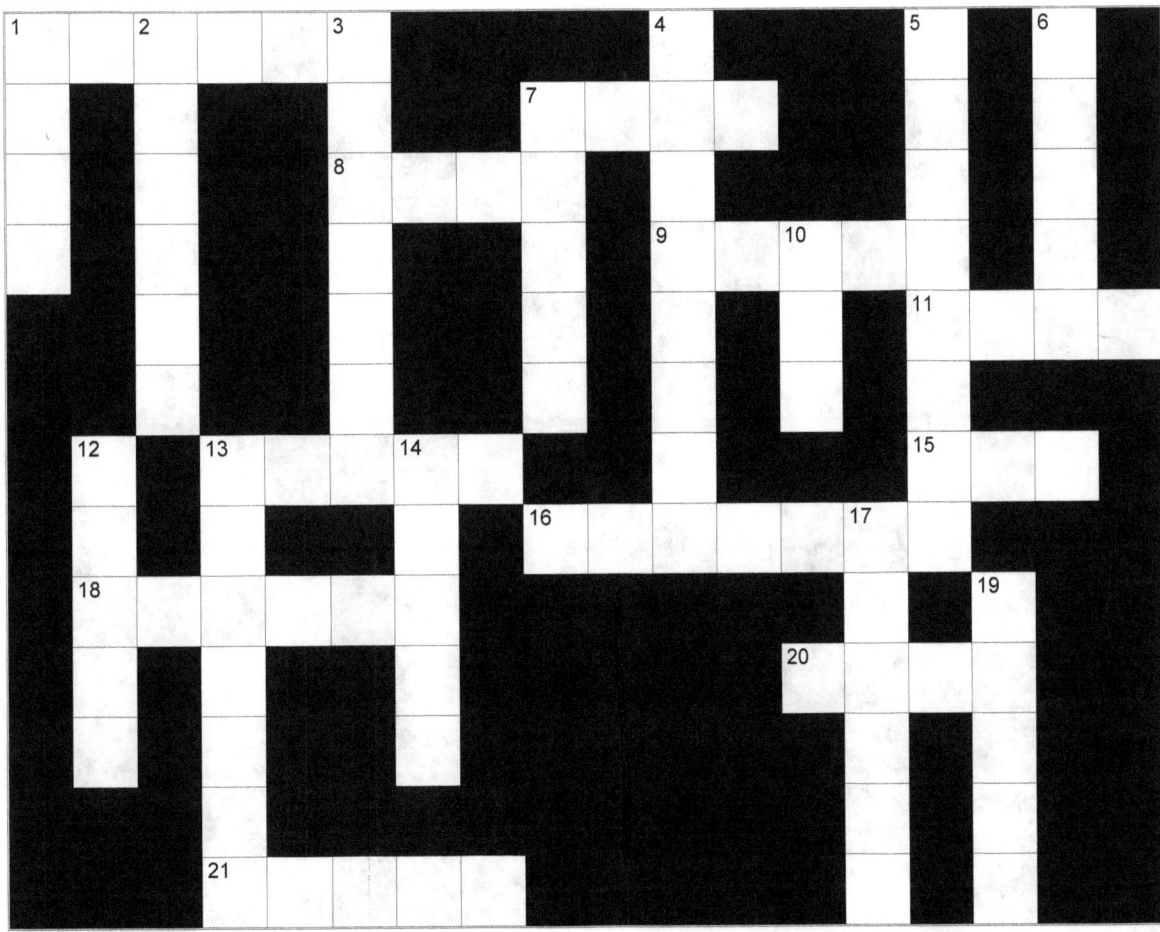

Across
1. The Palace of Green Porcelain
7. It attacked the Time Traveller in the far future; giant ___.
8. Name of the Journalist
9. Goes from 10:01 to 3:20 in just seconds
11. They had a peaceful, fruit-eating society.
13. Argumentative person with red hair
15. Eloi believed the Time Traveller came from this place.
16. People of the future had not seen these.
18. The Time Traveller compared the Eloi society to this.
20. Morlocks feared it.
21. They repositioned themselves over time.

Down
1. Eloi were this to the Morlocks.
2. Giant white statue in the forest
3. The ___ Man was instructed to begin dinner promptly at 7:00.
4. Time Traveller's housekeeper
5. The Time Traveller dreaded this.
6. The very young man wanted to hear Greek from ___'s lips.
7. Silent Man's name
10. Morlocks used this when cleaning the time machine.
12. Eloi survived on this food group.
13. Souvenir from the future; wilted ___
14. Editor's name
17. He spoke first after the Traveller's tale.
19. She nearly drowned.

Time Machine Crossword 1 Answer Key

	1 M	2 S	U	3 E	U	M			4 W			5 D		6 P
	E		P		E			7 C	R	A	B	A		L
	A		H		8 D	A	S	H		T		R		A
	T		I		I			O		9 C	10 L	O	C	K
			N		C			S		H		I	11 E	L	O	I
			X		A			E		E		L		N
	12 F	13 F	I	L	14 B	Y				T			15 S	U	N
	R	L			L		16 M	A	T	C	H	17 E	S	
	18 U	T	O	P	I	A						D		19 W
	I	W			N		20 F	I	R	E			
	T	E			K					T		E	
		R								O		N	
		21 S	T	A	R	S				R		A	

Across

1. The Palace of Green Porcelain
7. It attacked the Time Traveller in the far future; giant ___.
8. Name of the Journalist
9. Goes from 10:01 to 3:20 in just seconds
11. They had a peaceful, fruit-eating society.
13. Argumentative person with red hair
15. Eloi believed the Time Traveller came from this place.
16. People of the future had not seen these.
18. The Time Traveller compared the Eloi society to this.
20. Morlocks feared it.
21. They repositioned themselves over time.

Down

1. Eloi were this to the Morlocks.
2. Giant white statue in the forest
3. The ___ Man was instructed to begin dinner promptly at 7:00.
4. Time Traveller's housekeeper
5. The Time Traveller dreaded this.
6. The very young man wanted to hear Greek from ___'s lips.
7. Silent Man's name
10. Morlocks used this when cleaning the time machine.
12. Eloi survived on this food group.
13. Souvenir from the future; wilted ___
14. Editor's name
17. He spoke first after the Traveller's tale.
19. She nearly drowned.

Time Machine Crossword 2

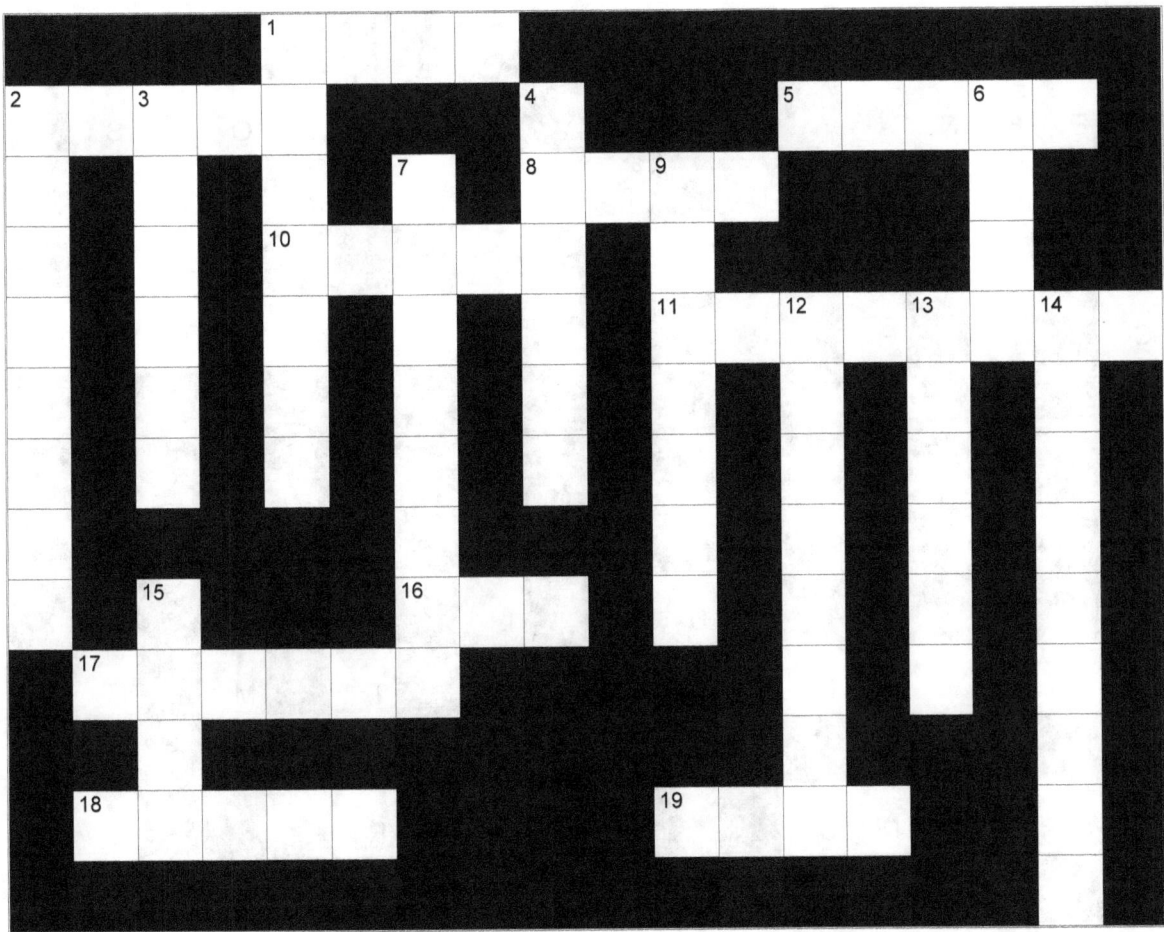

Across
1. It attacked the Time Traveller in the far future; giant ___.
2. She nearly drowned.
5. The Time Traveller threw these away when going through the forest with Weena.
8. The fourth dimension
10. The very young man wanted to hear Greek from ___'s lips.
11. Explosive the Time Traveller found in the museum
16. Eloi believed the Time Traveller came from this place.
17. The Time Traveller kept these in his pocket.
18. They repositioned themselves over time.
19. Morlocks feared it.

Down
1. Volatile substance the Time Traveller found in the museum
2. Time Traveller's housekeeper
3. He spoke first after the Traveller's tale.
4. The Time Traveller compared the Eloi society to this.
6. They had a peaceful, fruit-eating society.
7. The Time Traveller dreaded this.
9. The ___ Man was instructed to begin dinner promptly at 7:00.
12. He kept the Time Traveller's souvenir from the future.
13. The Palace of Green Porcelain
14. He found himself on a very strange adventure; the Time ___
15. Eloi were this to the Morlocks.

Time Machine Crossword 2 Answer Key

					1 C	R	A	B								
2 W	E	3 E	N	A			4 U			5 S	H	O	6 E	S		
A		D			7 D	8 T	I	9 M	E				L			
T		I	10 P	L	A	T	O						O			
C		T	H		R		P		11 D	12 Y	N	A	13 M	I	14 T	E
H		O	O		K		I		I	A			U		R	
E		R	R		E		A		C	R			S		A	
T					N				A	R			E		V	
T		15 M					16 S	U	N	A			U		E	
	17 L	E	V	E	R	S			L	T			M		L	
		A								O					L	
	18 S	T	A	R	S				19 F	I	R	E			E	
															R	

Across
1. It attacked the Time Traveller in the far future; giant ___.
2. She nearly drowned.
5. The Time Traveller threw these away when going through the forest with Weena.
8. The fourth dimension
10. The very young man wanted to hear Greek from ___'s lips.
11. Explosive the Time Traveller found in the museum
16. Eloi believed the Time Traveller came from this place.
17. The Time Traveller kept these in his pocket.
18. They repositioned themselves over time.
19. Morlocks feared it.

Down
1. Volatile substance the Time Traveller found in the museum
2. Time Traveller's housekeeper
3. He spoke first after the Traveller's tale.
4. The Time Traveller compared the Eloi society to this.
6. They had a peaceful, fruit-eating society.
7. The Time Traveller dreaded this.
9. The ___ Man was instructed to begin dinner promptly at 7:00.
12. He kept the Time Traveller's souvenir from the future.
13. The Palace of Green Porcelain
14. He found himself on a very strange adventure; the Time ___
15. Eloi were this to the Morlocks.

Time Machine Crossword 3

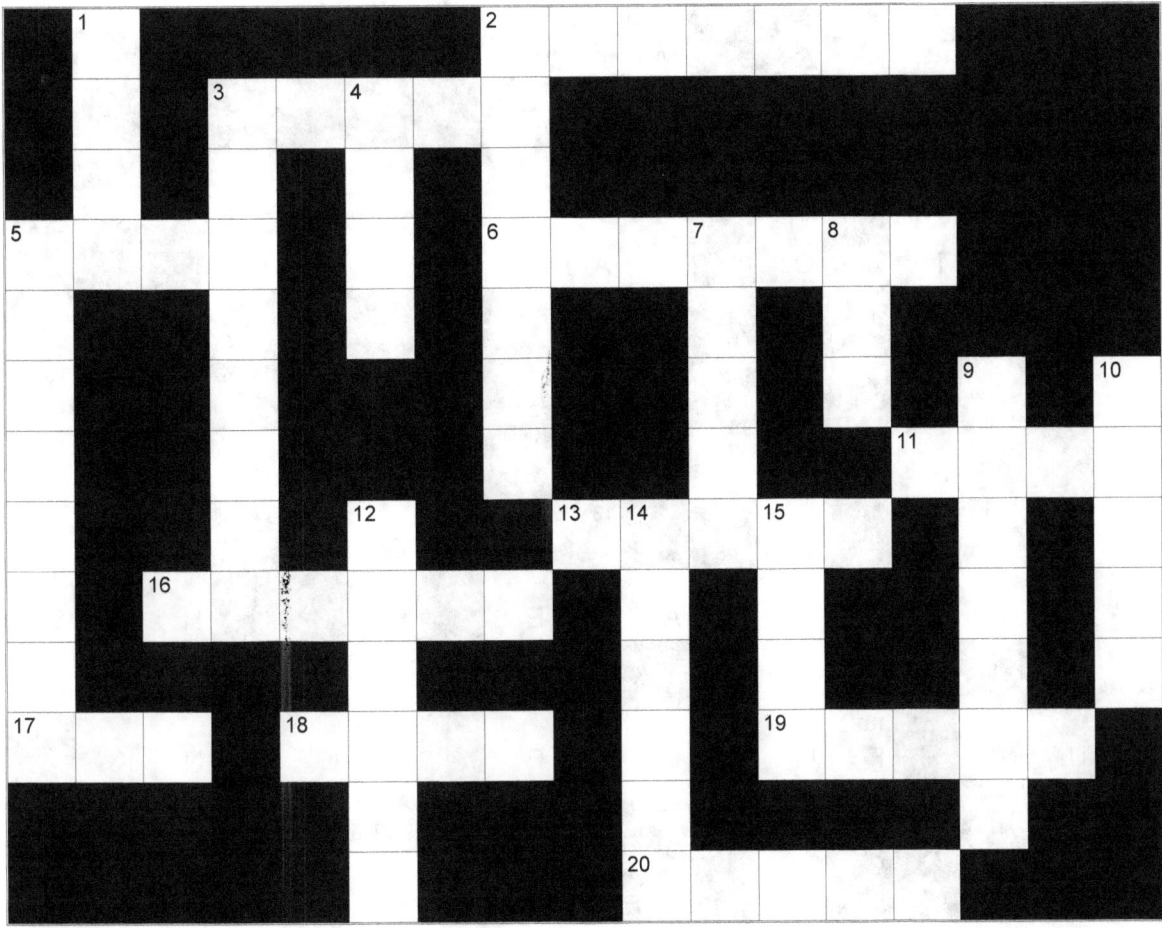

Across

2. The ___ Man was instructed to begin dinner promptly at 7:00.
3. She nearly drowned.
5. Eloi were this to the Morlocks.
6. Volatile substance the Time Traveller found in the museum
11. Name of the Journalist
13. Goes from 10:01 to 3:20 in just seconds
16. The Time Traveller compared the Eloi society to this.
17. Eloi believed the Time Traveller came from this place.
18. Morlocks feared it.
19. Editor's name
20. They repositioned themselves over time.

Down

1. The fourth dimension
2. People of the future had not seen these.
3. Time Traveller's housekeeper
4. They had a peaceful, fruit-eating society.
5. Industrious, underground carnivores
7. The very young man wanted to hear Greek from ___'s lips.
8. Morlocks used this when cleaning the time machine.
9. It was hidden inside the bronze pedestal.
10. Silent Man's name
12. Giant white statue in the forest
14. The Time Traveller kept these in his pocket.
15. It attacked the Time Traveller in the far future; giant ___.

Time Machine Crossword 3 Answer Key

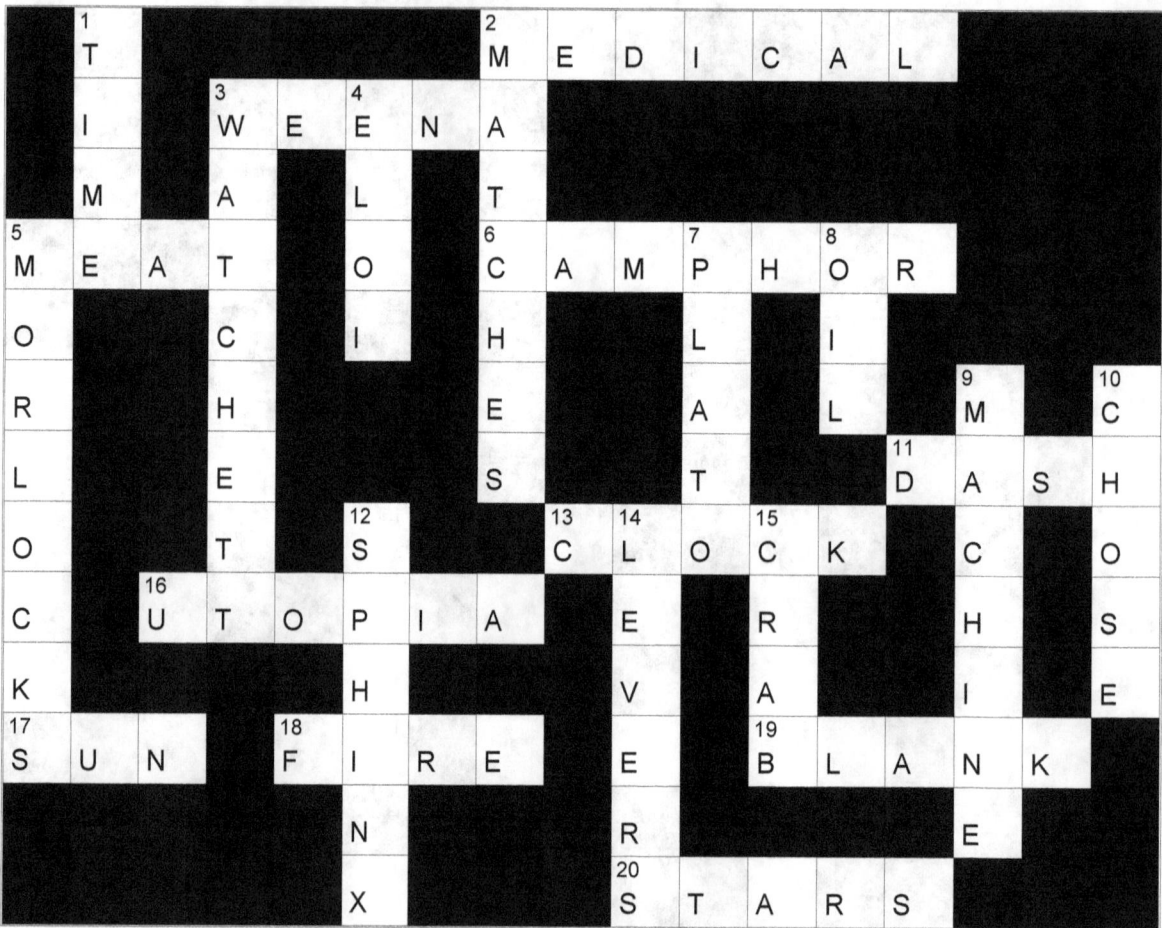

Across

2. The ___ Man was instructed to begin dinner promptly at 7:00.
3. She nearly drowned.
5. Eloi were this to the Morlocks.
6. Volatile substance the Time Traveller found in the museum
11. Name of the Journalist
13. Goes from 10:01 to 3:20 in just seconds
16. The Time Traveller compared the Eloi society to this.
17. Eloi believed the Time Traveller came from this place.
18. Morlocks feared it.
19. Editor's name
20. They repositioned themselves over time.

Down

1. The fourth dimension
2. People of the future had not seen these.
3. Time Traveller's housekeeper
4. They had a peaceful, fruit-eating society.
5. Industrious, underground carnivores
7. The very young man wanted to hear Greek from ___'s lips.
8. Morlocks used this when cleaning the time machine.
9. It was hidden inside the bronze pedestal.
10. Silent Man's name
12. Giant white statue in the forest
14. The Time Traveller kept these in his pocket.
15. It attacked the Time Traveller in the far future; giant ___.

Time Machine Crossword 4

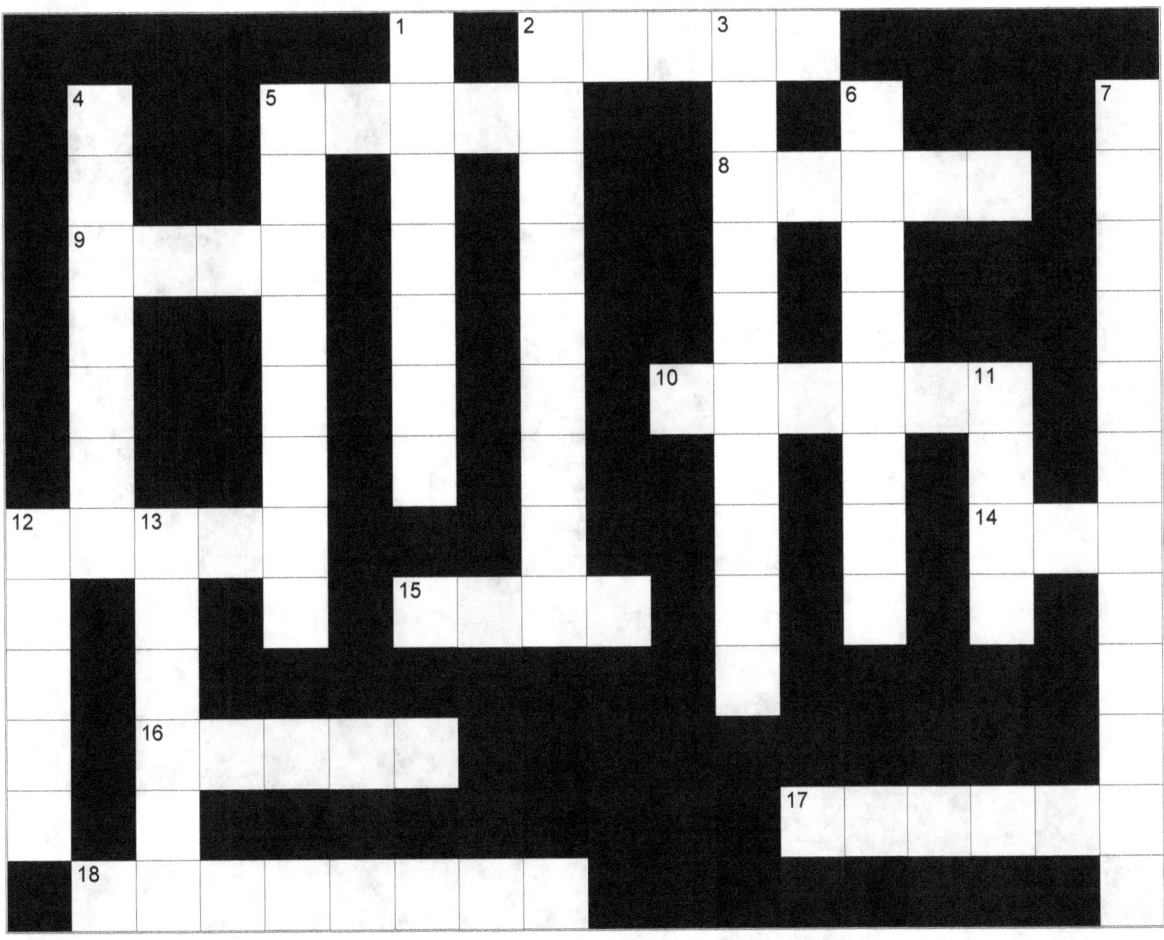

Across
2. They repositioned themselves over time.
5. She nearly drowned.
8. Goes from 10:01 to 3:20 in just seconds
9. Eloi were this to the Morlocks.
10. A clue as to where the time machine was hidden
12. Eloi survived on this food group.
14. Morlocks used this when cleaning the time machine.
15. Morlocks feared it.
16. The very young man wanted to hear Greek from ___'s lips.
17. The Time Traveller kept these in his pocket.
18. The Time Traveller dreaded this.

Down
1. The ___ Man was instructed to begin dinner promptly at 7:00.
2. The Time Traveller needs this to make gunpowder.
3. Publisher the Time Traveller never got to meet with
4. Volatile substance the Time Traveller found in the museum
5. Time Traveller's housekeeper
6. Industrious, underground carnivores
7. He presses the lever on the Time Machine model.
11. They had a peaceful, fruit-eating society.
12. Argumentative person with red hair
13. The Time Traveller compared the Eloi society to this.

Time Machine Crossword 4 Answer Key

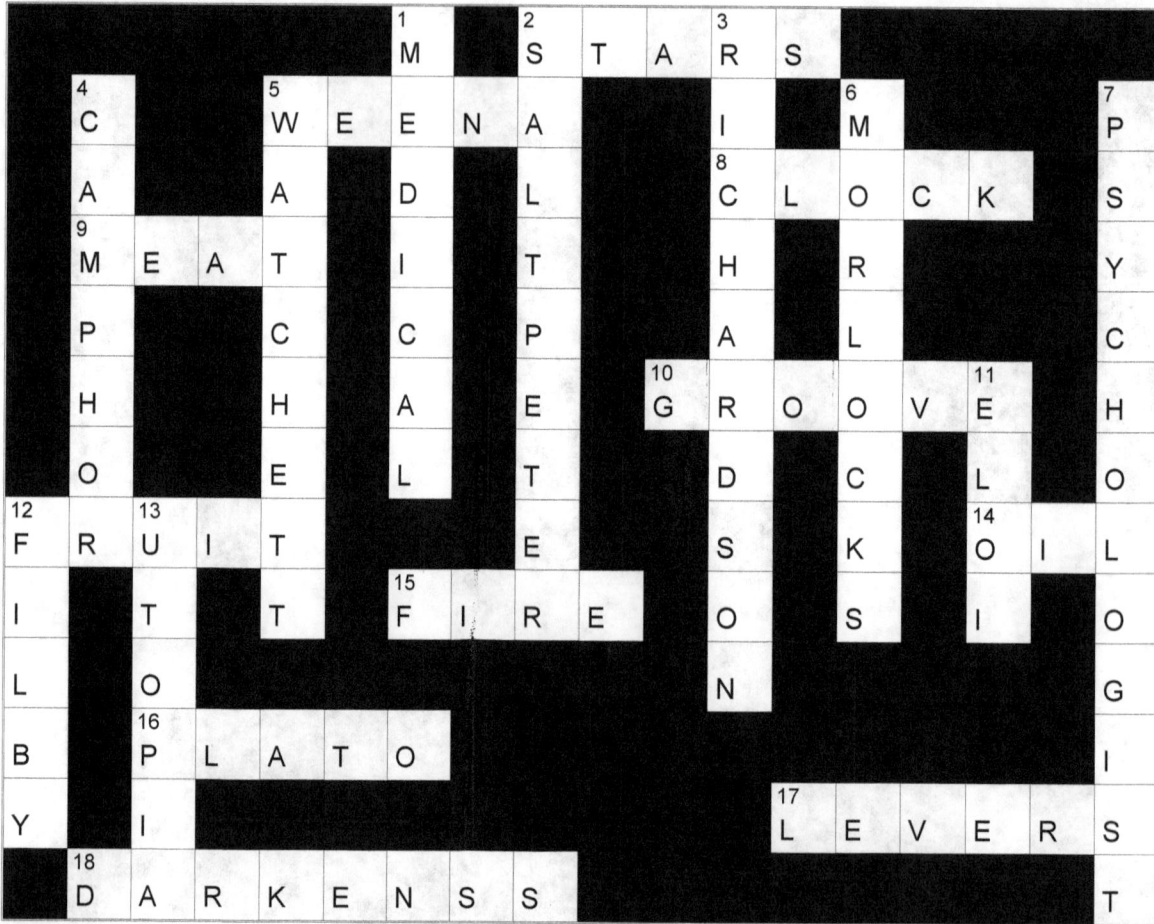

Across
2. They repositioned themselves over time.
5. She nearly drowned.
8. Goes from 10:01 to 3:20 in just seconds
9. Eloi were this to the Morlocks.
10. A clue as to where the time machine was hidden
12. Eloi survived on this food group.
14. Morlocks used this when cleaning the time machine.
15. Morlocks feared it.
16. The very young man wanted to hear Greek from ___'s lips.
17. The Time Traveller kept these in his pocket.
18. The Time Traveller dreaded this.

Down
1. The ___ Man was instructed to begin dinner promptly at 7:00.
2. The Time Traveller needs this to make gunpowder.
3. Publisher the Time Traveller never got to meet with
4. Volatile substance the Time Traveller found in the museum
5. Time Traveller's housekeeper
6. Industrious, underground carnivores
7. He presses the lever on the Time Machine model.
11. They had a peaceful, fruit-eating society.
12. Argumentative person with red hair
13. The Time Traveller compared the Eloi society to this.

Time Machine

GROOVE	STARS	PLATO	SILENT	GAZETTE
TRAVELLER	SPHINX	TIME	MEDICAL	EDITOR
MEAT	CHOSE	FREE SPACE	SHOES	FIRE
DARKENSS	SUN	FRUIT	ELOI	RHODODENDRON
CRAB	FILBY	MORLOCKS	MUSEUM	RICHARDSON

Time Machine

LEVERS	BLANK	DYNAMITE	CLOCK	NARRATOR
FLOWERS	DASH	MACHINE	WEENA	UTOPIA
CAMPHOR	OIL	FREE SPACE	WATCHETT	PSYCHOLOGIST
RICHARDSON	MUSEUM	MORLOCKS	FILBY	CRAB
RHODODENDRON	ELOI	FRUIT	SUN	DARKENSS

Time Machine

SHOES	LEVERS	WEENA	MORLOCKS	GROOVE
RICHARDSON	TRAVELLER	MUSEUM	SUN	UTOPIA
PSYCHOLOGIST	PLATO	FREE SPACE	CHOSE	WATCHETT
DYNAMITE	DARKENSS	ELOI	FLOWERS	CLOCK
CRAB	SALTPETER	SILENT	GAZETTE	RHODODENDRON

Time Machine

FILBY	FIRE	STARS	BLANK	CAMPHOR
TIME	EDITOR	MATCHES	NARRATOR	MEDICAL
SPHINX	OIL	FREE SPACE	FRUIT	MACHINE
RHODODENDRON	GAZETTE	SILENT	SALTPETER	CRAB
CLOCK	FLOWERS	ELOI	DARKENSS	DYNAMITE

Time Machine

SALTPETER	SPHINX	WEENA	UTOPIA	MACHINE
FRUIT	FIRE	SILENT	DYNAMITE	LEVERS
MEDICAL	BLANK	FREE SPACE	ELOI	MEAT
GROOVE	FILBY	SHOES	OIL	STARS
SUN	TIME	EDITOR	MORLOCKS	DARKENSS

Time Machine

FLOWERS	CHOSE	MUSEUM	WATCHETT	RICHARDSON
PLATO	CRAB	PSYCHOLOGIST	NARRATOR	CAMPHOR
RHODODENDRON	MATCHES	FREE SPACE	DASH	TRAVELLER
DARKENSS	MORLOCKS	EDITOR	TIME	SUN
STARS	OIL	SHOES	FILBY	GROOVE

Time Machine

TRAVELLER	OIL	CAMPHOR	SPHINX	BLANK
MUSEUM	MEDICAL	SUN	NARRATOR	DASH
WEENA	RICHARDSON	FREE SPACE	FRUIT	DARKENSS
MATCHES	UTOPIA	ELOI	SHOES	TIME
FILBY	PSYCHOLOGIST	LEVERS	GAZETTE	MORLOCKS

Time Machine

RHODODENDRON	GROOVE	STARS	MEAT	SALTPETER
MACHINE	CHOSE	CLOCK	SILENT	FLOWERS
PLATO	WATCHETT	FREE SPACE	FIRE	CRAB
MORLOCKS	GAZETTE	LEVERS	PSYCHOLOGIST	FILBY
TIME	SHOES	ELOI	UTOPIA	MATCHES

Time Machine

OIL	MUSEUM	RICHARDSON	DASH	NARRATOR
DARKENSS	FRUIT	SHOES	PLATO	MORLOCKS
GROOVE	RHODODENDRON	FREE SPACE	CHOSE	STARS
GAZETTE	MEAT	DYNAMITE	CAMPHOR	MEDICAL
SILENT	PSYCHOLOGIST	WATCHETT	FILBY	MATCHES

Time Machine

SALTPETER	TRAVELLER	EDITOR	SPHINX	BLANK
FLOWERS	CLOCK	UTOPIA	SUN	MACHINE
LEVERS	TIME	FREE SPACE	ELOI	CRAB
MATCHES	FILBY	WATCHETT	PSYCHOLOGIST	SILENT
MEDICAL	CAMPHOR	DYNAMITE	MEAT	GAZETTE

Time Machine

MEDICAL	RICHARDSON	MEAT	SHOES	CHOSE
BLANK	DASH	MACHINE	EDITOR	GAZETTE
WATCHETT	PSYCHOLOGIST	FREE SPACE	NARRATOR	CAMPHOR
PLATO	WEENA	FILBY	UTOPIA	ELOI
LEVERS	MORLOCKS	DARKENSS	TIME	OIL

Time Machine

DYNAMITE	FLOWERS	SUN	STARS	SALTPETER
FIRE	SILENT	MATCHES	RHODODENDRON	CLOCK
TRAVELLER	SPHINX	FREE SPACE	CRAB	FRUIT
OIL	TIME	DARKENSS	MORLOCKS	LEVERS
ELOI	UTOPIA	FILBY	WEENA	PLATO

Time Machine

FIRE	DASH	CRAB	CHOSE	MACHINE
FLOWERS	DYNAMITE	BLANK	MUSEUM	ELOI
RHODODENDRON	MATCHES	FREE SPACE	WATCHETT	RICHARDSON
UTOPIA	GAZETTE	NARRATOR	CLOCK	SHOES
OIL	SUN	MORLOCKS	EDITOR	FRUIT

Time Machine

SILENT	SALTPETER	CAMPHOR	GROOVE	PSYCHOLOGIST
STARS	TRAVELLER	MEAT	MEDICAL	PLATO
DARKENSS	WEENA	FREE SPACE	TIME	FILBY
FRUIT	EDITOR	MORLOCKS	SUN	OIL
SHOES	CLOCK	NARRATOR	GAZETTE	UTOPIA

Time Machine

SALTPETER	MEAT	RICHARDSON	FRUIT	PSYCHOLOGIST
WATCHETT	OIL	CHOSE	SILENT	DASH
FILBY	CLOCK	FREE SPACE	PLATO	SHOES
FIRE	MEDICAL	RHODODENDRON	GAZETTE	TIME
CAMPHOR	EDITOR	TRAVELLER	DARKENSS	UTOPIA

Time Machine

NARRATOR	CRAB	LEVERS	MACHINE	MATCHES
GROOVE	ELOI	BLANK	WEENA	MUSEUM
SPHINX	SUN	FREE SPACE	DYNAMITE	FLOWERS
UTOPIA	DARKENSS	TRAVELLER	EDITOR	CAMPHOR
TIME	GAZETTE	RHODODENDRON	MEDICAL	FIRE

Time Machine

FRUIT	GROOVE	PLATO	CHOSE	SILENT
PSYCHOLOGIST	TRAVELLER	STARS	MEAT	SHOES
FLOWERS	WATCHETT	FREE SPACE	WEENA	CLOCK
SALTPETER	RICHARDSON	ELOI	FILBY	MORLOCKS
OIL	MEDICAL	NARRATOR	EDITOR	DASH

Time Machine

SPHINX	CRAB	RHODODENDRON	DARKENSS	SUN
CAMPHOR	UTOPIA	DYNAMITE	LEVERS	GAZETTE
MUSEUM	MACHINE	FREE SPACE	FIRE	BLANK
DASH	EDITOR	NARRATOR	MEDICAL	OIL
MORLOCKS	FILBY	ELOI	RICHARDSON	SALTPETER

Time Machine

PSYCHOLOGIST	SILENT	OIL	SUN	DARKENSS
FRUIT	PLATO	MORLOCKS	RHODODENDRON	GAZETTE
EDITOR	TIME	FREE SPACE	DYNAMITE	WEENA
MUSEUM	UTOPIA	DASH	BLANK	CHOSE
WATCHETT	ELOI	NARRATOR	STARS	CLOCK

Time Machine

TRAVELLER	RICHARDSON	SALTPETER	MEAT	CRAB
FIRE	FLOWERS	CAMPHOR	LEVERS	MEDICAL
SHOES	GROOVE	FREE SPACE	MATCHES	MACHINE
CLOCK	STARS	NARRATOR	ELOI	WATCHETT
CHOSE	BLANK	DASH	UTOPIA	MUSEUM

Time Machine

LEVERS	RICHARDSON	PSYCHOLOGIST	UTOPIA	WATCHETT
MEAT	OIL	EDITOR	SUN	NARRATOR
RHODODENDRON	DYNAMITE	FREE SPACE	TIME	FLOWERS
SHOES	FILBY	STARS	MATCHES	FRUIT
GAZETTE	MUSEUM	SALTPETER	MEDICAL	PLATO

Time Machine

MACHINE	BLANK	CAMPHOR	GROOVE	SILENT
MORLOCKS	WEENA	CHOSE	SPHINX	DARKENSS
CLOCK	FIRE	FREE SPACE	DASH	CRAB
PLATO	MEDICAL	SALTPETER	MUSEUM	GAZETTE
FRUIT	MATCHES	STARS	FILBY	SHOES

Time Machine

MUSEUM	CAMPHOR	FILBY	BLANK	FIRE
UTOPIA	WEENA	PLATO	TRAVELLER	DYNAMITE
DARKENSS	RHODODENDRON	FREE SPACE	GAZETTE	MEDICAL
MEAT	NARRATOR	SUN	MORLOCKS	PSYCHOLOGIST
LEVERS	TIME	CLOCK	ELOI	SALTPETER

Time Machine

FRUIT	WATCHETT	SPHINX	EDITOR	CHOSE
MATCHES	MACHINE	OIL	STARS	DASH
RICHARDSON	SILENT	FREE SPACE	GROOVE	CRAB
SALTPETER	ELOI	CLOCK	TIME	LEVERS
PSYCHOLOGIST	MORLOCKS	SUN	NARRATOR	MEAT

Time Machine

ELOI	FIRE	DARKENSS	UTOPIA	FRUIT
FILBY	DASH	PSYCHOLOGIST	PLATO	SUN
OIL	CHOSE	FREE SPACE	RICHARDSON	DYNAMITE
GROOVE	FLOWERS	RHODODENDRON	CRAB	SALTPETER
CAMPHOR	SPHINX	LEVERS	GAZETTE	MEAT

Time Machine

WEENA	TRAVELLER	SILENT	MACHINE	TIME
EDITOR	STARS	BLANK	MATCHES	WATCHETT
SHOES	NARRATOR	FREE SPACE	MORLOCKS	CLOCK
MEAT	GAZETTE	LEVERS	SPHINX	CAMPHOR
SALTPETER	CRAB	RHODODENDRON	FLOWERS	GROOVE

Time Machine

OIL	DARKENSS	WATCHETT	MATCHES	SILENT
UTOPIA	LEVERS	MUSEUM	MEAT	SUN
PLATO	FIRE	FREE SPACE	SPHINX	SHOES
FRUIT	RICHARDSON	MACHINE	TIME	GAZETTE
DYNAMITE	CHOSE	PSYCHOLOGIST	CRAB	CLOCK

Time Machine

RHODODENDRON	FLOWERS	CAMPHOR	DASH	NARRATOR
WEENA	MEDICAL	ELOI	EDITOR	FILBY
SALTPETER	MORLOCKS	FREE SPACE	TRAVELLER	BLANK
CLOCK	CRAB	PSYCHOLOGIST	CHOSE	DYNAMITE
GAZETTE	TIME	MACHINE	RICHARDSON	FRUIT

Time Machine

GROOVE	FLOWERS	DARKENSS	MEAT	BLANK
DASH	EDITOR	MUSEUM	LEVERS	GAZETTE
TRAVELLER	CRAB	FREE SPACE	SUN	ELOI
NARRATOR	SILENT	MACHINE	DYNAMITE	WATCHETT
FIRE	WEENA	SHOES	PSYCHOLOGIST	FILBY

Time Machine

MATCHES	MEDICAL	CAMPHOR	SALTPETER	CHOSE
STARS	RHODODENDRON	SPHINX	CLOCK	OIL
RICHARDSON	MORLOCKS	FREE SPACE	UTOPIA	TIME
FILBY	PSYCHOLOGIST	SHOES	WEENA	FIRE
WATCHETT	DYNAMITE	MACHINE	SILENT	NARRATOR

Time Machine

SALTPETER	GROOVE	LEVERS	CHOSE	WATCHETT
MUSEUM	MEDICAL	SPHINX	STARS	FLOWERS
TIME	FIRE	FREE SPACE	FILBY	MATCHES
RHODODENDRON	SUN	DARKENSS	MORLOCKS	DASH
BLANK	GAZETTE	TRAVELLER	FRUIT	EDITOR

Time Machine

WEENA	RICHARDSON	CRAB	CAMPHOR	OIL
NARRATOR	ELOI	SILENT	MACHINE	CLOCK
UTOPIA	PSYCHOLOGIST	FREE SPACE	PLATO	MEAT
EDITOR	FRUIT	TRAVELLER	GAZETTE	BLANK
DASH	MORLOCKS	DARKENSS	SUN	RHODODENDRON

Time Machine Vocabulary Word List

TIME MACHINE VOCABULARY

No.	Word	Clue/Definition
1.	ABOMINATIONS	Things that cause a sense of disgust
2.	ACACIAS	Fragrant yellow flowers used in perfumes
3.	ALGAL	Relating to algae
4.	AMELIORATING	Making better, more bearable, or more satisfactory
5.	ANACHRONISMS	Persons, objects, or practices that belong to a different time period
6.	ANECDOTES	Short accounts of interesting or humorous incidents
7.	APERTURE	Opening, as a hole, slit, crack, or gap
8.	ATTENUATED	Made thin
9.	BEGRIMED	Dirty
10.	BOLE	Stem or trunk of a tree
11.	CALAMITY	Great misfortune or disaster
12.	CAMPHOR	Compound used in the manufacture of plastics and explosives
13.	COLOSSAL	Huge
14.	COMPENSATION	Given or received in return for services or debt
15.	CONTRIVANCE	Device or control that is useful for a particular job
16.	CUPOLAS	Small domes set on a round base or resting on pillars
17.	DECADENT	In a condition or process of mental or moral decay
18.	DELIQUESCED	Became liquid by absorbing moisture from the air
19.	DILAPIDATED	Fallen into partial ruin or decay, as from age, wear, or neglect
20.	EDDYING	Swirling as if in a whirlpool
21.	EKING	Getting with great effort or strain
22.	ELUDE	Avoid or escape by speed, cleverness or trickery
23.	FRUGIVOROUS	Feeding on fruit; fruit-eating
24.	GAUDY	Brilliantly or excessively showy
25.	IMPARTIALITY	Showing no bias; neutrality
26.	IMPEDED	Slowed or obstructed the progress of
27.	INARTICULATE	Lacking the ability to express oneself, esp. in clear speech
28.	INCREDULOUS	Showing unbelief; skeptical
29.	INDOLENT	Showing a disposition to avoid exertion; lazy
30.	INTERMINABLE	Unending
31.	INTIMATE	To indicate or make known indirectly; hint; imply; suggest
32.	MACE	Club-like, armor-breaking weapon of war
33.	MEEK	Overly submissive or compliant; spiritless; tame
34.	MUTTON	The meat of sheep
35.	PALLID	Pale; faint or deficient in color
36.	PEPTONE	Complex water-soluble nutrient obtained by digesting protein
37.	PHANTASM	Creation of the imagination or fancy; fantasy
38.	POIGNANT	Affecting or moving the emotions
39.	PRECESSIONAL	Slow, conical motion of the earth's axis of rotation
40.	PRECOCIOUS	Unusually advanced or mature in development, esp. mentally
41.	PRETERNATURALLY	Out of the ordinary course of nature; exceptionally or abnormally
42.	PRODIGIOUS	Extraordinary in size, amount, extent, degree, force, etc.
43.	RECEDED	Moved away from; retreated; withdrew
44.	RECONDITE	Dealing with very profound or difficult subject matter
45.	RILL	Small brook; rivulet

Time Machine Vocabulary Word List

No. Word	Clue/Definition
46. SAURIANS	Lizards or similar reptiles
47. SHOAL	Sandbank or sand bar in a body of water exposed at low tide
48. SLACKENED	Made or became slower; slowed down
49. SPECTRAL	Ghostly
50. SUCCULENT	Full of juice; juicy
51. TEMERITY	Reckless boldness; rashness
52. TETHERED	Confined or restricted with or as if with a rope or chain
53. TRUNCATED	Shortened by or as if by having a part cut off; cut short
54. TUMULT	Highly distressing agitation of mind or feeling
55. VELOCITY	Rapidity of motion or operation; swiftness; speed
56. VERDIGRIS	Blue-green crust formed on copper, brass, or bronze surfaces
57. WAN	Unnatural or sickly pallor; pallid; lacking color
58. WHIM	Odd or capricious notion or desire; a sudden fancy

Time Machine Vocabulary Fill In The Blanks 1

_____

_____

_____

_____

_____

_____

_____

_____

_____

_____

_____

_____

_____

_____

_____

_____

_____

_____

_____

_____

1. Reckless boldness; rashness
2. Made thin
3. Blue-green crust formed on copper, brass, or bronze surfaces
4. Club-like, armor-breaking weapon of war
5. Highly distressing agitation of mind or feeling
6. Great misfortune or disaster
7. Device or control that is useful for a particular job
8. Odd or capricious notion or desire; a sudden fancy
9. Showing a disposition to avoid exertion; lazy
10. Small brook; rivulet
11. Huge
12. Slowed or obstructed the progress of
13. Given or received in return for services or debt
14. Relating to algae
15. Pale; faint or deficient in color
16. Showing unbelief; skeptical
17. Short accounts of interesting or humorous incidents
18. Fallen into partial ruin or decay, as from age, wear, or neglect
19. Avoid or escape by speed, cleverness or trickery
20. Dealing with very profound or difficult subject matter

Time Machine Vocabulary Fill In The Blanks 1 Answer Key

TEMERITY	1. Reckless boldness; rashness
ATTENUATED	2. Made thin
VERDIGRIS	3. Blue-green crust formed on copper, brass, or bronze surfaces
MACE	4. Club-like, armor-breaking weapon of war
TUMULT	5. Highly distressing agitation of mind or feeling
CALAMITY	6. Great misfortune or disaster
CONTRIVANCE	7. Device or control that is useful for a particular job
WHIM	8. Odd or capricious notion or desire; a sudden fancy
INDOLENT	9. Showing a disposition to avoid exertion; lazy
RILL	10. Small brook; rivulet
COLOSSAL	11. Huge
IMPEDED	12. Slowed or obstructed the progress of
COMPENSATION	13. Given or received in return for services or debt
ALGAL	14. Relating to algae
PALLID	15. Pale; faint or deficient in color
INCREDULOUS	16. Showing unbelief; skeptical
ANECDOTES	17. Short accounts of interesting or humorous incidents
DILAPIDATED	18. Fallen into partial ruin or decay, as from age, wear, or neglect
ELUDE	19. Avoid or escape by speed, cleverness or trickery
RECONDITE	20. Dealing with very profound or difficult subject matter

Time Machine Vocabulary Fill In The Blanks 2

_____

_____

_____

_____

_____

_____

_____

_____

_____

_____

_____

_____

_____

_____

_____

_____

_____

_____

_____

_____

1. Extraordinary in size, amount, extent, degree, force, etc.
2. Fragrant yellow flowers used in perfumes
3. Club-like, armor-breaking weapon of war
4. Slow, conical motion of the earth's axis of rotation
5. Unnatural or sickly pallor; pallid; lacking color
6. Feeding on fruit; fruit-eating
7. Small brook; rivulet
8. Given or received in return for services or debt
9. Making better, more bearable, or more satisfactory
10. Unusually advanced or mature in development, esp. mentally
11. Lacking the ability to express oneself, esp. in clear speech
12. Dirty
13. Slowed or obstructed the progress of
14. Became liquid by absorbing moisture from the air
15. Out of the ordinary course of nature; exceptionally or abnormally
16. Rapidity of motion or operation; swiftness; speed
17. Unending
18. Odd or capricious notion or desire; a sudden fancy
19. Overly submissive or compliant; spiritless; tame
20. Relating to algae

Time Machine Vocabulary Fill In The Blanks 2 Answer Key

PRODIGIOUS	1. Extraordinary in size, amount, extent, degree, force, etc.
ACACIAS	2. Fragrant yellow flowers used in perfumes
MACE	3. Club-like, armor-breaking weapon of war
PRECESSIONAL	4. Slow, conical motion of the earth's axis of rotation
WAN	5. Unnatural or sickly pallor; pallid; lacking color
FRUGIVOROUS	6. Feeding on fruit; fruit-eating
RILL	7. Small brook; rivulet
COMPENSATION	8. Given or received in return for services or debt
AMELIORATING	9. Making better, more bearable, or more satisfactory
PRECOCIOUS	10. Unusually advanced or mature in development, esp. mentally
INARTICULATE	11. Lacking the ability to express oneself, esp. in clear speech
BEGRIMED	12. Dirty
IMPEDED	13. Slowed or obstructed the progress of
DELIQUESCED	14. Became liquid by absorbing moisture from the air
PRETERNATURALLY	15. Out of the ordinary course of nature; exceptionally or abnormally
VELOCITY	16. Rapidity of motion or operation; swiftness; speed
INTERMINABLE	17. Unending
WHIM	18. Odd or capricious notion or desire; a sudden fancy
MEEK	19. Overly submissive or compliant; spiritless; tame
ALGAL	20. Relating to algae

Time Machine Vocabulary Fill In The Blanks 3

_____

1. Great misfortune or disaster
2. Shortened by or as if by having a part cut off; cut short
3. Reckless boldness; rashness
4. Slow, conical motion of the earth's axis of rotation
5. Unending
6. Unusually advanced or mature in development, esp. mentally
7. Overly submissive or compliant; spiritless; tame
8. Huge
9. Sandbank or sand bar in a body of water exposed at low tide
10. Unnatural or sickly pallor; pallid; lacking color
11. Showing unbelief; skeptical
12. Became liquid by absorbing moisture from the air
13. Lacking the ability to express oneself, esp. in clear speech
14. Fallen into partial ruin or decay, as from age, wear, or neglect
15. Ghostly
16. Out of the ordinary course of nature; exceptionally or abnormally
17. Made thin
18. Things that cause a sense of disgust
19. Feeding on fruit; fruit-eating
20. Confined or restricted with or as if with a rope or chain

Time Machine Vocabulary Fill In The Blanks 3 Answer Key

CALAMITY	1. Great misfortune or disaster
TRUNCATED	2. Shortened by or as if by having a part cut off; cut short
TEMERITY	3. Reckless boldness; rashness
PRECESSIONAL	4. Slow, conical motion of the earth's axis of rotation
INTERMINABLE	5. Unending
PRECOCIOUS	6. Unusually advanced or mature in development, esp. mentally
MEEK	7. Overly submissive or compliant; spiritless; tame
COLOSSAL	8. Huge
SHOAL	9. Sandbank or sand bar in a body of water exposed at low tide
WAN	10. Unnatural or sickly pallor; pallid; lacking color
INCREDULOUS	11. Showing unbelief; skeptical
DELIQUESCED	12. Became liquid by absorbing moisture from the air
INARTICULATE	13. Lacking the ability to express oneself, esp. in clear speech
DILAPIDATED	14. Fallen into partial ruin or decay, as from age, wear, or neglect
SPECTRAL	15. Ghostly
PRETERNATURALLY	16. Out of the ordinary course of nature; exceptionally or abnormally
ATTENUATED	17. Made thin
ABOMINATIONS	18. Things that cause a sense of disgust
FRUGIVOROUS	19. Feeding on fruit; fruit-eating
TETHERED	20. Confined or restricted with or as if with a rope or chain

Time Machine Vocabulary Fill In The Blanks 4

1. Small domes set on a round base or resting on pillars
2. Slowed or obstructed the progress of
3. In a condition or process of mental or moral decay
4. Compound used in the manufacture of plastics and explosives
5. Reckless boldness; rashness
6. Making better, more bearable, or more satisfactory
7. Moved away from; retreated; withdrew
8. Showing a disposition to avoid exertion; lazy
9. Dealing with very profound or difficult subject matter
10. Given or received in return for services or debt
11. Persons, objects, or practices that belong to a different time period
12. Sandbank or sand bar in a body of water exposed at low tide
13. Things that cause a sense of disgust
14. Fallen into partial ruin or decay, as from age, wear, or neglect
15. The meat of sheep
16. Huge
17. Shortened by or as if by having a part cut off; cut short
18. Slow, conical motion of the earth's axis of rotation
19. Odd or capricious notion or desire; a sudden fancy
20. To indicate or make known indirectly; hint; imply; suggest

Time Machine Vocabulary Fill In The Blanks 4 Answer Key

CUPOLAS	1. Small domes set on a round base or resting on pillars
IMPEDED	2. Slowed or obstructed the progress of
DECADENT	3. In a condition or process of mental or moral decay
CAMPHOR	4. Compound used in the manufacture of plastics and explosives
TEMERITY	5. Reckless boldness; rashness
AMELIORATING	6. Making better, more bearable, or more satisfactory
RECEDED	7. Moved away from; retreated; withdrew
INDOLENT	8. Showing a disposition to avoid exertion; lazy
RECONDITE	9. Dealing with very profound or difficult subject matter
COMPENSATION	10. Given or received in return for services or debt
ANACHRONISMS	11. Persons, objects, or practices that belong to a different time period
SHOAL	12. Sandbank or sand bar in a body of water exposed at low tide
ABOMINATIONS	13. Things that cause a sense of disgust
DILAPIDATED	14. Fallen into partial ruin or decay, as from age, wear, or neglect
MUTTON	15. The meat of sheep
COLOSSAL	16. Huge
TRUNCATED	17. Shortened by or as if by having a part cut off; cut short
PRECESSIONAL	18. Slow, conical motion of the earth's axis of rotation
WHIM	19. Odd or capricious notion or desire; a sudden fancy
INTIMATE	20. To indicate or make known indirectly; hint; imply; suggest

Time Machine Vocabulary Matching 1

___ 1. ATTENUATED   A. Sandbank or sand bar in a body of water exposed at low tide
___ 2. BOLE   B. Affecting or moving the emotions
___ 3. POIGNANT   C. Persons, objects, or practices that belong to a different time period
___ 4. CALAMITY   D. Things that cause a sense of disgust
___ 5. VELOCITY   E. Small domes set on a round base or resting on pillars
___ 6. APERTURE   F. Made thin
___ 7. EDDYING   G. Making better, more bearable, or more satisfactory
___ 8. SLACKENED   H. Opening, as a hole, slit, crack, or gap
___ 9. SPECTRAL   I. Overly submissive or compliant; spiritless; tame
___10. ABOMINATIONS   J. Made or became slower; slowed down
___11. IMPEDED   K. Creation of the imagination or fancy; fantasy
___12. COLOSSAL   L. Given or received in return for services or debt
___13. INTERMINABLE   M. Rapidity of motion or operation; swiftness; speed
___14. MEEK   N. Out of the ordinary course of nature; exceptionally or abnormally
___15. IMPARTIALITY   O. Showing no bias; neutrality
___16. ANACHRONISMS   P. Lizards or similar reptiles
___17. CUPOLAS   Q. Short accounts of interesting or humorous incidents
___18. AMELIORATING   R. Ghostly
___19. ANECDOTES   S. Unending
___20. SAURIANS   T. Huge
___21. ACACIAS   U. Swirling as if in a whirlpool
___22. PRETERNATURALLY   V. Slowed or obstructed the progress of
___23. SHOAL   W. Fragrant yellow flowers used in perfumes
___24. COMPENSATION   X. Great misfortune or disaster
___25. PHANTASM   Y. Stem or trunk of a tree

Time Machine Vocabulary Matching 1 Answer Key

F - 1. ATTENUATED		A. Sandbank or sand bar in a body of water exposed at low tide
Y - 2. BOLE		B. Affecting or moving the emotions
B - 3. POIGNANT		C. Persons, objects, or practices that belong to a different time period
X - 4. CALAMITY		D. Things that cause a sense of disgust
M - 5. VELOCITY		E. Small domes set on a round base or resting on pillars
H - 6. APERTURE		F. Made thin
U - 7. EDDYING		G. Making better, more bearable, or more satisfactory
J - 8. SLACKENED		H. Opening, as a hole, slit, crack, or gap
R - 9. SPECTRAL		I. Overly submissive or compliant; spiritless; tame
D - 10. ABOMINATIONS		J. Made or became slower; slowed down
V - 11. IMPEDED		K. Creation of the imagination or fancy; fantasy
T - 12. COLOSSAL		L. Given or received in return for services or debt
S - 13. INTERMINABLE		M. Rapidity of motion or operation; swiftness; speed
I - 14. MEEK		N. Out of the ordinary course of nature; exceptionally or abnormally
O - 15. IMPARTIALITY		O. Showing no bias; neutrality
C - 16. ANACHRONISMS		P. Lizards or similar reptiles
E - 17. CUPOLAS		Q. Short accounts of interesting or humorous incidents
G - 18. AMELIORATING		R. Ghostly
Q - 19. ANECDOTES		S. Unending
P - 20. SAURIANS		T. Huge
W - 21. ACACIAS		U. Swirling as if in a whirlpool
N - 22. PRETERNATURALLY		V. Slowed or obstructed the progress of
A - 23. SHOAL		W. Fragrant yellow flowers used in perfumes
L - 24. COMPENSATION		X. Great misfortune or disaster
K - 25. PHANTASM		Y. Stem or trunk of a tree

Time Machine Vocabulary Matching 2

___ 1. ELUDE
___ 2. SLACKENED
___ 3. RILL
___ 4. EKING
___ 5. ACACIAS
___ 6. RECEDED
___ 7. TEMERITY
___ 8. IMPARTIALITY
___ 9. PRECOCIOUS
___ 10. ANACHRONISMS
___ 11. PEPTONE
___ 12. BOLE
___ 13. COMPENSATION
___ 14. VELOCITY
___ 15. PRECESSIONAL
___ 16. INCREDULOUS
___ 17. DECADENT
___ 18. MACE
___ 19. VERDIGRIS
___ 20. COLOSSAL
___ 21. INARTICULATE
___ 22. MEEK
___ 23. RECONDITE
___ 24. MUTTON
___ 25. WHIM

A. Given or received in return for services or debt
B. Slow, conical motion of the earth's axis of rotation
C. Reckless boldness; rashness
D. Fragrant yellow flowers used in perfumes
E. Unusually advanced or mature in development, esp. mentally
F. Huge
G. Showing no bias; neutrality
H. Persons, objects, or practices that belong to a different time period
I. Complex water-soluble nutrient obtained by digesting protein
J. Odd or capricious notion or desire; a sudden fancy
K. Moved away from; retreated; withdrew
L. Getting with great effort or strain
M. Made or became slower; slowed down
N. Blue-green crust formed on copper, brass, or bronze surfaces
O. Showing unbelief; skeptical
P. Club-like, armor-breaking weapon of war
Q. Stem or trunk of a tree
R. Dealing with very profound or difficult subject matter
S. Lacking the ability to express oneself, esp. in clear speech
T. Avoid or escape by speed, cleverness or trickery
U. The meat of sheep
V. Overly submissive or compliant; spiritless; tame
W. Rapidity of motion or operation; swiftness; speed
X. In a condition or process of mental or moral decay
Y. Small brook; rivulet

Time Machine Vocabulary Matching 2 Answer Key

T - 1. ELUDE
M - 2. SLACKENED
Y - 3. RILL
L - 4. EKING
D - 5. ACACIAS
K - 6. RECEDED
C - 7. TEMERITY
G - 8. IMPARTIALITY
E - 9. PRECOCIOUS
H - 10. ANACHRONISMS
I - 11. PEPTONE
Q - 12. BOLE
A - 13. COMPENSATION
W - 14. VELOCITY
B - 15. PRECESSIONAL
O - 16. INCREDULOUS
X - 17. DECADENT
P - 18. MACE
N - 19. VERDIGRIS
F - 20. COLOSSAL
S - 21. INARTICULATE
V - 22. MEEK
R - 23. RECONDITE
U - 24. MUTTON
J - 25. WHIM

A. Given or received in return for services or debt
B. Slow, conical motion of the earth's axis of rotation
C. Reckless boldness; rashness
D. Fragrant yellow flowers used in perfumes
E. Unusually advanced or mature in development, esp. mentally
F. Huge
G. Showing no bias; neutrality
H. Persons, objects, or practices that belong to a different time period
I. Complex water-soluble nutrient obtained by digesting protein
J. Odd or capricious notion or desire; a sudden fancy
K. Moved away from; retreated; withdrew
L. Getting with great effort or strain
M. Made or became slower; slowed down
N. Blue-green crust formed on copper, brass, or bronze surfaces
O. Showing unbelief; skeptical
P. Club-like, armor-breaking weapon of war
Q. Stem or trunk of a tree
R. Dealing with very profound or difficult subject matter
S. Lacking the ability to express oneself, esp. in clear speech
T. Avoid or escape by speed, cleverness or trickery
U. The meat of sheep
V. Overly submissive or compliant; spiritless; tame
W. Rapidity of motion or operation; swiftness; speed
X. In a condition or process of mental or moral decay
Y. Small brook; rivulet

Time Machine Vocabulary Matching 3

___ 1. EKING
___ 2. DELIQUESCED
___ 3. PRODIGIOUS
___ 4. FRUGIVOROUS
___ 5. COMPENSATION
___ 6. SAURIANS
___ 7. PEPTONE
___ 8. INARTICULATE
___ 9. WAN
___ 10. ATTENUATED
___ 11. PRETERNATURALLY
___ 12. DILAPIDATED
___ 13. CALAMITY
___ 14. INTIMATE
___ 15. TEMERITY
___ 16. RECONDITE
___ 17. TRUNCATED
___ 18. INDOLENT
___ 19. SHOAL
___ 20. ACACIAS
___ 21. ELUDE
___ 22. INTERMINABLE
___ 23. TETHERED
___ 24. APERTURE
___ 25. ABOMINATIONS

A. Out of the ordinary course of nature; exceptionally or abnormally
B. Extraordinary in size, amount, extent, degree, force, etc.
C. To indicate or make known indirectly; hint; imply; suggest
D. Given or received in return for services or debt
E. Things that cause a sense of disgust
F. Lacking the ability to express oneself, esp. in clear speech
G. Feeding on fruit; fruit-eating
H. Became liquid by absorbing moisture from the air
I. Sandbank or sand bar in a body of water exposed at low tide
J. Showing a disposition to avoid exertion; lazy
K. Reckless boldness; rashness
L. Unnatural or sickly pallor; pallid; lacking color
M. Confined or restricted with or as if with a rope or chain
N. Dealing with very profound or difficult subject matter
O. Opening, as a hole, slit, crack, or gap
P. Getting with great effort or strain
Q. Avoid or escape by speed, cleverness or trickery
R. Shortened by or as if by having a part cut off; cut short
S. Unending
T. Fallen into partial ruin or decay, as from age, wear, or neglect
U. Great misfortune or disaster
V. Complex water-soluble nutrient obtained by digesting protein
W. Fragrant yellow flowers used in perfumes
X. Lizards or similar reptiles
Y. Made thin

Time Machine Vocabulary Matching 3 Answer Key

P - 1. EKING	A. Out of the ordinary course of nature; exceptionally or abnormally
H - 2. DELIQUESCED	B. Extraordinary in size, amount, extent, degree, force, etc.
B - 3. PRODIGIOUS	C. To indicate or make known indirectly; hint; imply; suggest
G - 4. FRUGIVOROUS	D. Given or received in return for services or debt
D - 5. COMPENSATION	E. Things that cause a sense of disgust
X - 6. SAURIANS	F. Lacking the ability to express oneself, esp. in clear speech
V - 7. PEPTONE	G. Feeding on fruit; fruit-eating
F - 8. INARTICULATE	H. Became liquid by absorbing moisture from the air
L - 9. WAN	I. Sandbank or sand bar in a body of water exposed at low tide
Y - 10. ATTENUATED	J. Showing a disposition to avoid exertion; lazy
A - 11. PRETERNATURALLY	K. Reckless boldness; rashness
T - 12. DILAPIDATED	L. Unnatural or sickly pallor; pallid; lacking color
U - 13. CALAMITY	M. Confined or restricted with or as if with a rope or chain
C - 14. INTIMATE	N. Dealing with very profound or difficult subject matter
K - 15. TEMERITY	O. Opening, as a hole, slit, crack, or gap
N - 16. RECONDITE	P. Getting with great effort or strain
R - 17. TRUNCATED	Q. Avoid or escape by speed, cleverness or trickery
J - 18. INDOLENT	R. Shortened by or as if by having a part cut off; cut short
I - 19. SHOAL	S. Unending
W - 20. ACACIAS	T. Fallen into partial ruin or decay, as from age, wear, or neglect
Q - 21. ELUDE	U. Great misfortune or disaster
S - 22. INTERMINABLE	V. Complex water-soluble nutrient obtained by digesting protein
M - 23. TETHERED	W. Fragrant yellow flowers used in perfumes
O - 24. APERTURE	X. Lizards or similar reptiles
E - 25. ABOMINATIONS	Y. Made thin

Time Machine Vocabulary Matching 4

___ 1. MUTTON
___ 2. SUCCULENT
___ 3. AMELIORATING
___ 4. RILL
___ 5. DECADENT
___ 6. INARTICULATE
___ 7. IMPEDED
___ 8. SAURIANS
___ 9. BEGRIMED
___ 10. DELIQUESCED
___ 11. VERDIGRIS
___ 12. ALGAL
___ 13. ANACHRONISMS
___ 14. PHANTASM
___ 15. SPECTRAL
___ 16. ACACIAS
___ 17. APERTURE
___ 18. ATTENUATED
___ 19. CONTRIVANCE
___ 20. RECEDED
___ 21. TUMULT
___ 22. ANECDOTES
___ 23. VELOCITY
___ 24. INDOLENT
___ 25. PRODIGIOUS

A. Moved away from; retreated; withdrew
B. Made thin
C. Small brook; rivulet
D. Short accounts of interesting or humorous incidents
E. Relating to algae
F. Slowed or obstructed the progress of
G. In a condition or process of mental or moral decay
H. Extraordinary in size, amount, extent, degree, force, etc.
I. Creation of the imagination or fancy; fantasy
J. Fragrant yellow flowers used in perfumes
K. Lizards or similar reptiles
L. Making better, more bearable, or more satisfactory
M. Opening, as a hole, slit, crack, or gap
N. Persons, objects, or practices that belong to a different time period
O. The meat of sheep
P. Became liquid by absorbing moisture from the air
Q. Highly distressing agitation of mind or feeling
R. Dirty
S. Device or control that is useful for a particular job
T. Showing a disposition to avoid exertion; lazy
U. Ghostly
V. Blue-green crust formed on copper, brass, or bronze surfaces
W. Rapidity of motion or operation; swiftness; speed
X. Lacking the ability to express oneself, esp. in clear speech
Y. Full of juice; juicy

Time Machine Vocabulary Matching 4 Answer Key

O - 1. MUTTON		A. Moved away from; retreated; withdrew
Y - 2. SUCCULENT		B. Made thin
L - 3. AMELIORATING		C. Small brook; rivulet
C - 4. RILL		D. Short accounts of interesting or humorous incidents
G - 5. DECADENT		E. Relating to algae
X - 6. INARTICULATE		F. Slowed or obstructed the progress of
F - 7. IMPEDED		G. In a condition or process of mental or moral decay
K - 8. SAURIANS		H. Extraordinary in size, amount, extent, degree, force, etc.
R - 9. BEGRIMED		I. Creation of the imagination or fancy; fantasy
P - 10. DELIQUESCED		J. Fragrant yellow flowers used in perfumes
V - 11. VERDIGRIS		K. Lizards or similar reptiles
E - 12. ALGAL		L. Making better, more bearable, or more satisfactory
N - 13. ANACHRONISMS		M. Opening, as a hole, slit, crack, or gap
I - 14. PHANTASM		N. Persons, objects, or practices that belong to a different time period
U - 15. SPECTRAL		O. The meat of sheep
J - 16. ACACIAS		P. Became liquid by absorbing moisture from the air
M - 17. APERTURE		Q. Highly distressing agitation of mind or feeling
B - 18. ATTENUATED		R. Dirty
S - 19. CONTRIVANCE		S. Device or control that is useful for a particular job
A - 20. RECEDED		T. Showing a disposition to avoid exertion; lazy
Q - 21. TUMULT		U. Ghostly
D - 22. ANECDOTES		V. Blue-green crust formed on copper, brass, or bronze surfaces
W - 23. VELOCITY		W. Rapidity of motion or operation; swiftness; speed
T - 24. INDOLENT		X. Lacking the ability to express oneself, esp. in clear speech
H - 25. PRODIGIOUS		Y. Full of juice; juicy

Time Machine Vocabulary Magic Squares 1

Match the definition with the vocabulary word. Put your answers in the magic squares below. When your answers are correct, all columns and rows will add to the same number.

A. VERDIGRIS
B. CAMPHOR
C. BEGRIMED
D. ELUDE
E. DELIQUESCED
F. DILAPIDATED
G. ALGAL
H. PEPTONE
I. RECONDITE
J. CALAMITY
K. EKING
L. IMPEDED
M. ATTENUATED
N. VELOCITY
O. DECADENT
P. RECEDED

1. Compound used in the manufacture of plastics and explosives
2. Relating to algae
3. Getting with great effort or strain
4. Rapidity of motion or operation; swiftness; speed
5. Made thin
6. Slowed or obstructed the progress of
7. Complex water-soluble nutrient obtained by digesting protein
8. Blue-green crust formed on copper, brass, or bronze surfaces
9. Moved away from; retreated; withdrew
10. Dealing with very profound or difficult subject matter
11. Became liquid by absorbing moisture from the air
12. Avoid or escape by speed, cleverness or trickery
13. Dirty
14. Fallen into partial ruin or decay, as from age, wear, or neglect
15. Great misfortune or disaster
16. In a condition or process of mental or moral decay

A=	B=	C=	D=
E=	F=	G=	H=
I=	J=	K=	L=
M=	N=	O=	P=

Time Machine Vocabulary Magic Squares 1 Answer Key

Match the definition with the vocabulary word. Put your answers in the magic squares below. When your answers are correct, all columns and rows will add to the same number.

A. VERDIGRIS
B. CAMPHOR
C. BEGRIMED
D. ELUDE
E. DELIQUESCED
F. DILAPIDATED
G. ALGAL
H. PEPTONE
I. RECONDITE
J. CALAMITY
K. EKING
L. IMPEDED
M. ATTENUATED
N. VELOCITY
O. DECADENT
P. RECEDED

1. Compound used in the manufacture of plastics and explosives
2. Relating to algae
3. Getting with great effort or strain
4. Rapidity of motion or operation; swiftness; speed
5. Made thin
6. Slowed or obstructed the progress of
7. Complex water-soluble nutrient obtained by digesting protein
8. Blue-green crust formed on copper, brass, or bronze surfaces
9. Moved away from; retreated; withdrew
10. Dealing with very profound or difficult subject matter
11. Became liquid by absorbing moisture from the air
12. Avoid or escape by speed, cleverness or trickery
13. Dirty
14. Fallen into partial ruin or decay, as from age, wear, or neglect
15. Great misfortune or disaster
16. In a condition or process of mental or moral decay

A=8	B=1	C=13	D=12
E=11	F=14	G=2	H=7
I=10	J=15	K=3	L=6
M=5	N=4	O=16	P=9

Time Machine Vocabulary Magic Squares 2

Match the definition with the vocabulary word. Put your answers in the magic squares below. When your answers are correct, all columns and rows will add to the same number.

A. DECADENT
B. ALGAL
C. PALLID
D. MUTTON
E. CALAMITY
F. PHANTASM
G. RECONDITE
H. ABOMINATIONS
I. TEMERITY
J. CAMPHOR
K. IMPARTIALITY
L. SPECTRAL
M. PEPTONE
N. ELUDE
O. COLOSSAL
P. INARTICULATE

1. Complex water-soluble nutrient obtained by digesting protein
2. Creation of the imagination or fancy; fantasy
3. Things that cause a sense of disgust
4. Huge
5. Ghostly
6. Pale; faint or deficient in color
7. In a condition or process of mental or moral decay
8. Compound used in the manufacture of plastics and explosives
9. Showing no bias; neutrality
10. The meat of sheep
11. Relating to algae
12. Reckless boldness; rashness
13. Avoid or escape by speed, cleverness or trickery
14. Great misfortune or disaster
15. Dealing with very profound or difficult subject matter
16. Lacking the ability to express oneself, esp. in clear speech

A=	B=	C=	D=
E=	F=	G=	H=
I=	J=	K=	L=
M=	N=	O=	P=

Time Machine Vocabulary Magic Squares 2 Answer Key

Match the definition with the vocabulary word. Put your answers in the magic squares below. When your answers are correct, all columns and rows will add to the same number.

A. DECADENT
B. ALGAL
C. PALLID
D. MUTTON
E. CALAMITY
F. PHANTASM
G. RECONDITE
H. ABOMINATIONS
I. TEMERITY
J. CAMPHOR
K. IMPARTIALITY
L. SPECTRAL
M. PEPTONE
N. ELUDE
O. COLOSSAL
P. INARTICULATE

1. Complex water-soluble nutrient obtained by digesting protein
2. Creation of the imagination or fancy; fantasy
3. Things that cause a sense of disgust
4. Huge
5. Ghostly
6. Pale; faint or deficient in color
7. In a condition or process of mental or moral decay
8. Compound used in the manufacture of plastics and explosives
9. Showing no bias; neutrality
10. The meat of sheep
11. Relating to algae
12. Reckless boldness; rashness
13. Avoid or escape by speed, cleverness or trickery
14. Great misfortune or disaster
15. Dealing with very profound or difficult subject matter
16. Lacking the ability to express oneself, esp. in clear speech

A=7	B=11	C=6	D=10
E=14	F=2	G=15	H=3
I=12	J=8	K=9	L=5
M=1	N=13	O=4	P=16

Time Machine Vocabulary Magic Squares 3

Match the definition with the vocabulary word. Put your answers in the magic squares below. When your answers are correct, all columns and rows will add to the same number.

A. BEGRIMED
B. DECADENT
C. SLACKENED
D. MUTTON
E. COLOSSAL
F. INTERMINABLE
G. CAMPHOR
H. CUPOLAS
I. SPECTRAL
J. PRETERNATURALLY
K. CONTRIVANCE
L. TRUNCATED
M. ANECDOTES
N. SHOAL
O. EKING
P. POIGNANT

1. Small domes set on a round base or resting on pillars
2. Dirty
3. In a condition or process of mental or moral decay
4. Compound used in the manufacture of plastics and explosives
5. Out of the ordinary course of nature; exceptionally or abnormally
6. Getting with great effort or strain
7. Affecting or moving the emotions
8. Ghostly
9. Device or control that is useful for a particular job
10. Sandbank or sand bar in a body of water exposed at low tide
11. Short accounts of interesting or humorous incidents
12. Shortened by or as if by having a part cut off; cut short
13. Huge
14. The meat of sheep
15. Made or became slower; slowed down
16. Unending

A=	B=	C=	D=
E=	F=	G=	H=
I=	J=	K=	L=
M=	N=	O=	P=

Time Machine Vocabulary Magic Squares 3 Answer Key

Match the definition with the vocabulary word. Put your answers in the magic squares below. When your answers are correct, all columns and rows will add to the same number.

A. BEGRIMED
B. DECADENT
C. SLACKENED
D. MUTTON
E. COLOSSAL
F. INTERMINABLE
G. CAMPHOR
H. CUPOLAS
I. SPECTRAL
J. PRETERNATURALLY
K. CONTRIVANCE
L. TRUNCATED
M. ANECDOTES
N. SHOAL
O. EKING
P. POIGNANT

1. Small domes set on a round base or resting on pillars
2. Dirty
3. In a condition or process of mental or moral decay
4. Compound used in the manufacture of plastics and explosives
5. Out of the ordinary course of nature; exceptionally or abnormally
6. Getting with great effort or strain
7. Affecting or moving the emotions
8. Ghostly
9. Device or control that is useful for a particular job
10. Sandbank or sand bar in a body of water exposed at low tide
11. Short accounts of interesting or humorous incidents
12. Shortened by or as if by having a part cut off; cut short
13. Huge
14. The meat of sheep
15. Made or became slower; slowed down
16. Unending

A=2	B=3	C=15	D=14
E=13	F=16	G=4	H=1
I=8	J=5	K=9	L=12
M=11	N=10	O=6	P=7

Time Machine Vocabulary Magic Squares 4

Match the definition with the vocabulary word. Put your answers in the magic squares below. When your answers are correct, all columns and rows will add to the same number.

A. PRECOCIOUS
B. SHOAL
C. WHIM
D. ANECDOTES
E. COLOSSAL
F. ATTENUATED
G. DILAPIDATED
H. RECEDED
I. PHANTASM
J. TUMULT
K. VERDIGRIS
L. RILL
M. TEMERITY
N. INCREDULOUS
O. CUPOLAS
P. ELUDE

1. Small domes set on a round base or resting on pillars
2. Short accounts of interesting or humorous incidents
3. Highly distressing agitation of mind or feeling
4. Huge
5. Creation of the imagination or fancy; fantasy
6. Made thin
7. Avoid or escape by speed, cleverness or trickery
8. Odd or capricious notion or desire; a sudden fancy
9. Moved away from; retreated; withdrew
10. Blue-green crust formed on copper, brass, or bronze surfaces
11. Unusually advanced or mature in development, esp. mentally
12. Showing unbelief; skeptical
13. Sandbank or sand bar in a body of water exposed at low tide
14. Reckless boldness; rashness
15. Fallen into partial ruin or decay, as from age, wear, or neglect
16. Small brook; rivulet

A=	B=	C=	D=
E=	F=	G=	H=
I=	J=	K=	L=
M=	N=	O=	P=

Time Machine Vocabulary Magic Squares 4 Answer Key

Match the definition with the vocabulary word. Put your answers in the magic squares below. When your answers are correct, all columns and rows will add to the same number.

A. PRECOCIOUS
B. SHOAL
C. WHIM
D. ANECDOTES
E. COLOSSAL
F. ATTENUATED
G. DILAPIDATED
H. RECEDED
I. PHANTASM
J. TUMULT
K. VERDIGRIS
L. RILL
M. TEMERITY
N. INCREDULOUS
O. CUPOLAS
P. ELUDE

1. Small domes set on a round base or resting on pillars
2. Short accounts of interesting or humorous incidents
3. Highly distressing agitation of mind or feeling
4. Huge
5. Creation of the imagination or fancy; fantasy
6. Made thin
7. Avoid or escape by speed, cleverness or trickery
8. Odd or capricious notion or desire; a sudden fancy
9. Moved away from; retreated; withdrew
10. Blue-green crust formed on copper, brass, or bronze surfaces
11. Unusually advanced or mature in development, esp. mentally
12. Showing unbelief; skeptical
13. Sandbank or sand bar in a body of water exposed at low tide
14. Reckless boldness; rashness
15. Fallen into partial ruin or decay, as from age, wear, or neglect
16. Small brook; rivulet

A=11	B=13	C=8	D=2
E=4	F=6	G=15	H=9
I=5	J=3	K=10	L=16
M=14	N=12	O=1	P=7

Time Machine Vocabulary Word Search 1

```
D I L L A P S J H S C K Q D K S B E D M
B N X S X C X X I D U G H E C N M K E G
E D M P V C A R X K P G K D R A T I L K
T O N E N S G C Q T O M C E O I G N I D
A L T C B I P Q I R L P K P H R M G Q X
M E F T D X E Z I A A T Z M P U B E U T
I N C R E D U L O U S W H I M A C E E G
T T E A U Z L H U T P D A S A S R L S K
N V B L P G S M D D E O A N C T O A C S
I T E M E R I T Y T E T I T L B G G E M
X T G U Y N H V A N N R H G U V B L D F
C T R T R Y H U O A T G E E N M W A D V
P J I T M V N V H R Z X A C R A U L X W
K S M O R E F P Z K O F J U E E N L Z R
W F E N T N E L U C C U S L D D D T T C
N R D T C O L O S S A L S X N Y E M K K
D C A L A M I T Y S L A C K E N E D P B
```

Affecting or moving the emotions (8)
Avoid or escape by speed, cleverness or trickery (5)
Became liquid by absorbing moisture from the air (11)
Blue-green crust formed on copper, brass, or bronze surfaces (9)
Brilliantly or excessively showy (5)
Club-like, armor-breaking weapon of war (4)
Compound used in the manufacture of plastics and explosives (7)
Confined or restricted with or as if with a rope or chain (8)
Creation of the imagination or fancy; fantasy (8)
Dirty (8)
Feeding on fruit; fruit-eating (11)
Fragrant yellow flowers used in perfumes (7)
Full of juice; juicy (9)
Getting with great effort or strain (5)
Ghostly (8)
Great misfortune or disaster (8)
Highly distressing agitation of mind or feeling (6)
Huge (8)

Lizards or similar reptiles (8)
Made or became slower; slowed down (9)
Made thin (10)
Moved away from; retreated; withdrew (7)
Odd or capricious notion or desire; a sudden fancy (4)
Overly submissive or compliant; spiritless; tame (4)
Pale; faint or deficient in color (6)
Reckless boldness; rashness (8)
Relating to algae (5)
Sandbank or sand bar in a body of water exposed at low tide (5)
Showing a disposition to avoid exertion; lazy (8)
Showing unbelief; skeptical (11)
Slowed or obstructed the progress of (7)
Small brook; rivulet (4)
Small domes set on a round base or resting on pillars (7)
Stem or trunk of a tree (4)
The meat of sheep (6)
To indicate or make known indirectly; hint; imply; suggest (8)
Unnatural or sickly pallor; pallid; lacking color (3)

Time Machine Vocabulary Word Search 1 Answer Key

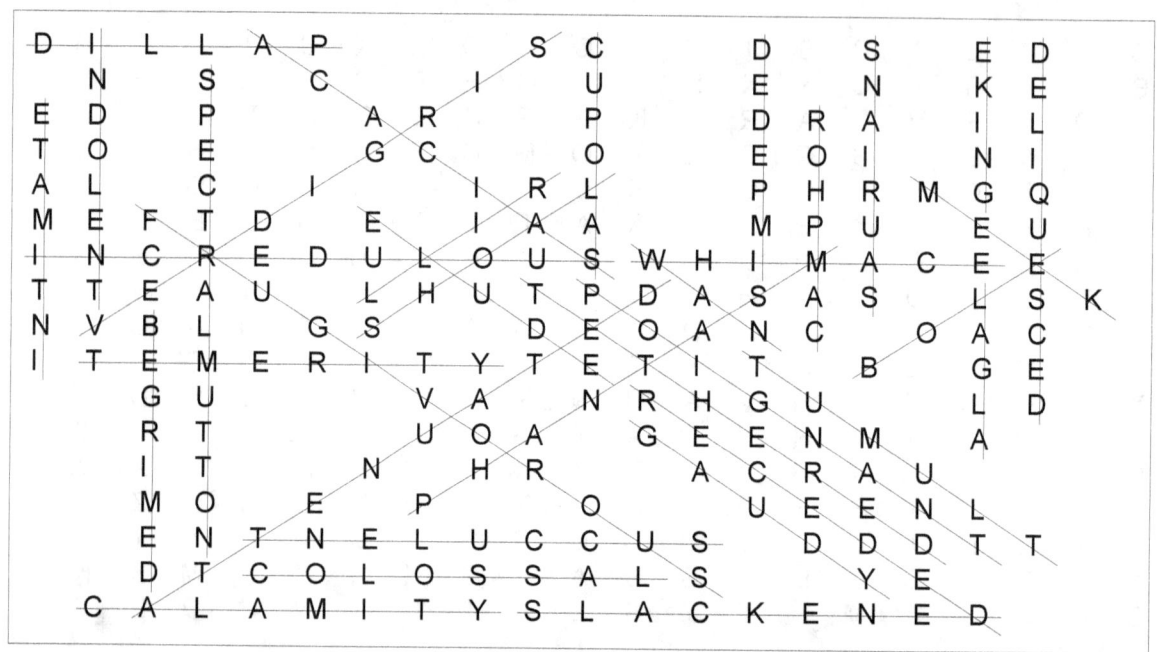

Affecting or moving the emotions (8)
Avoid or escape by speed, cleverness or trickery (5)
Became liquid by absorbing moisture from the air (11)
Blue-green crust formed on copper, brass, or bronze surfaces (9)
Brilliantly or excessively showy (5)
Club-like, armor-breaking weapon of war (4)
Compound used in the manufacture of plastics and explosives (7)
Confined or restricted with or as if with a rope or chain (8)
Creation of the imagination or fancy; fantasy (8)
Dirty (8)
Feeding on fruit; fruit-eating (11)
Fragrant yellow flowers used in perfumes (7)
Full of juice; juicy (9)
Getting with great effort or strain (5)
Ghostly (8)
Great misfortune or disaster (8)
Highly distressing agitation of mind or feeling (6)
Huge (8)

Lizards or similar reptiles (8)
Made or became slower; slowed down (9)
Made thin (10)
Moved away from; retreated; withdrew (7)
Odd or capricious notion or desire; a sudden fancy (4)
Overly submissive or compliant; spiritless; tame (4)
Pale; faint or deficient in color (6)
Reckless boldness; rashness (8)
Relating to algae (5)
Sandbank or sand bar in a body of water exposed at low tide (5)
Showing a disposition to avoid exertion; lazy (8)
Showing unbelief; skeptical (11)
Slowed or obstructed the progress of (7)
Small brook; rivulet (4)
Small domes set on a round base or resting on pillars (7)
Stem or trunk of a tree (4)
The meat of sheep (6)
To indicate or make known indirectly; hint; imply; suggest (8)
Unnatural or sickly pallor; pallid; lacking color (3)

Time Machine Vocabulary Word Search 2

M	U	T	T	O	N	V	E	R	D	I	G	R	I	S	D	F	R	P	M
N	I	H	J	B	C	S	L	D	E	T	A	C	N	U	R	T	E	E	J
Y	S	N	A	I	R	U	A	S	J	T	E	B	P	W	K	D	C	P	L
T	A	P	T	Y	I	C	P	K	L	N	R	M	P	R	J	F	E	T	Q
I	P	P	A	I	Z	M	W	O	G	E	J	Z	E	D	B	L	D	O	P
L	E	Z	G	L	M	X	P	B	L	D	R	M	E	R	M	G	E	N	Z
A	R	P	S	H	L	A	Q	E	K	A	V	C	S	H	I	P	D	E	Q
I	T	H	Q	T	X	I	T	Y	D	C	S	K	C	N	B	T	R	Z	B
T	U	M	U	L	T	S	D	E	N	E	K	C	A	L	S	O	Y	L	T
R	R	S	C	Y	A	U	C	V	U	D	D	W	L	E	H	Z	L	G	J
A	E	H	G	I	A	A	E	Q	M	T	D	F	A	P	L	R	V	E	H
P	H	O	C	G	M	L	I	B	E	G	R	I	M	E	D	U	I	N	C
M	L	A	S	S	O	L	O	C	E	V	M	A	I	E	N	V	D	L	F
I	C	L	P	C	E	A	W	Q	K	I	C	L	T	X	K	H	Z	E	L
A	F	Z	I	D	G	G	B	R	H	T	P	S	Y	S	V	I	X	Y	C
Q	P	T	X	V	J	L	L	W	M	N	K	E	D	D	Y	I	N	G	W
T	Y	L	H	Y	W	A	T	S	P	E	C	T	R	A	L	G	V	G	P

Avoid or escape by speed, cleverness or trickery (5)
Became liquid by absorbing moisture from the air (11)
Blue-green crust formed on copper, brass, or bronze surfaces (9)
Brilliantly or excessively showy (5)
Club-like, armor-breaking weapon of war (4)
Complex water-soluble nutrient obtained by digesting protein (7)
Compound used in the manufacture of plastics and explosives (7)
Dirty (8)
Fragrant yellow flowers used in perfumes (7)
Getting with great effort or strain (5)
Ghostly (8)
Great misfortune or disaster (8)
Highly distressing agitation of mind or feeling (6)
Huge (8)
In a condition or process of mental or moral decay (8)
Lizards or similar reptiles (8)
Made or became slower; slowed down (9)
Moved away from; retreated; withdrew (7)

Odd or capricious notion or desire; a sudden fancy (4)
Opening, as a hole, slit, crack, or gap (8)
Overly submissive or compliant; spiritless; tame (4)
Pale; faint or deficient in color (6)
Rapidity of motion or operation; swiftness; speed (8)
Reckless boldness; rashness (8)
Relating to algae (5)
Sandbank or sand bar in a body of water exposed at low tide (5)
Shortened by or as if by having a part cut off; cut short (9)
Showing no bias; neutrality (12)
Slowed or obstructed the progress of (7)
Small brook; rivulet (4)
Small domes set on a round base or resting on pillars (7)
Stem or trunk of a tree (4)
Swirling as if in a whirlpool (7)
The meat of sheep (6)
To indicate or make known indirectly; hint; imply; suggest (8)
Unnatural or sickly pallor; pallid; lacking color (3)

Time Machine Vocabulary Word Search 2 Answer Key

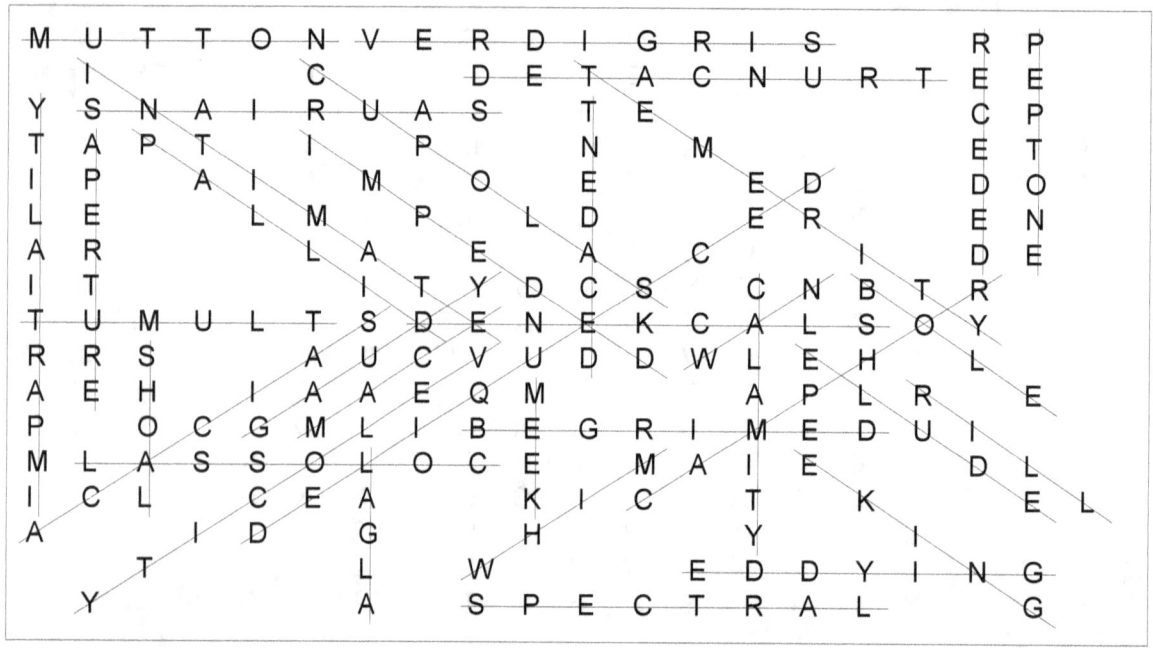

Avoid or escape by speed, cleverness or trickery (5)
Became liquid by absorbing moisture from the air (11)
Blue-green crust formed on copper, brass, or bronze surfaces (9)
Brilliantly or excessively showy (5)
Club-like, armor-breaking weapon of war (4)
Complex water-soluble nutrient obtained by digesting protein (7)
Compound used in the manufacture of plastics and explosives (7)
Dirty (8)
Fragrant yellow flowers used in perfumes (7)
Getting with great effort or strain (5)
Ghostly (8)
Great misfortune or disaster (8)
Highly distressing agitation of mind or feeling (6)
Huge (8)
In a condition or process of mental or moral decay (8)
Lizards or similar reptiles (8)
Made or became slower; slowed down (9)
Moved away from; retreated; withdrew (7)

Odd or capricious notion or desire; a sudden fancy (4)
Opening, as a hole, slit, crack, or gap (8)
Overly submissive or compliant; spiritless; tame (4)
Pale; faint or deficient in color (6)
Rapidity of motion or operation; swiftness; speed (8)
Reckless boldness; rashness (8)
Relating to algae (5)
Sandbank or sand bar in a body of water exposed at low tide (5)
Shortened by or as if by having a part cut off; cut short (9)
Showing no bias; neutrality (12)
Slowed or obstructed the progress of (7)
Small brook; rivulet (4)
Small domes set on a round base or resting on pillars (7)
Stem or trunk of a tree (4)
Swirling as if in a whirlpool (7)
The meat of sheep (6)
To indicate or make known indirectly; hint; imply; suggest (8)
Unnatural or sickly pallor; pallid; lacking color (3)

Time Machine Vocabulary Word Search 3

```
P R E C O C I O U S C A Y I M P E D E D D
S B N O L T D D B A U N T P C S M W R H
U S O L V P E E I P E I H A A B Z U Q
C G T O E S C R G C O C L A M U B R T D
C W P S R N A E R A L D A N P R I S R X
U V E S D O D H I C A O I T H I N P E C
L D P A I I E T M A S T T A O A T E P L
E E J L G T N E E F B E R S R N I C A B
N N D T R A T T D M B S A M B S M T P C
T E E N I N U G T H E M P W E T A R P Y
T K T E S I D D M T U R M T H Z T A L L
T C A L A M I T Y T E K I N G M E L G Y
V A C O E O Y V T C E D W T V L T N P L
N L N D L B L O E E N M H P Y L I S A Q
M S U N W A N D M O R A I K U Y E H L Q
C L R I G L E S C T I C M M D L B O L W
E Q T L Q D B E K S L E U D O S M A I V
Z Q A W T G R N T N L T E B V Y F L D H
```

ABOMINATIONS
ACACIAS
ALGAL
ANECDOTES
APERTURE
BEGRIMED
BOLE
CALAMITY
CAMPHOR
COLOSSAL
CUPOLAS
DECADENT
EDDYING
EKING

ELUDE
GAUDY
IMPARTIALITY
IMPEDED
INDOLENT
INTIMATE
MACE
MEEK
MUTTON
PALLID
PEPTONE
PHANTASM
PRECOCIOUS
RECEDED

RECONDITE
RILL
SAURIANS
SHOAL
SLACKENED
SPECTRAL
SUCCULENT
TEMERITY
TETHERED
TRUNCATED
TUMULT
VERDIGRIS
WAN
WHIM

Time Machine Vocabulary Word Search 3 Answer Key

[word search grid]

ABOMINATIONS	ELUDE	RECONDITE
ACACIAS	GAUDY	RILL
ALGAL	IMPARTIALITY	SAURIANS
ANECDOTES	IMPEDED	SHOAL
APERTURE	INDOLENT	SLACKENED
BEGRIMED	INTIMATE	SPECTRAL
BOLE	MACE	SUCCULENT
CALAMITY	MEEK	TEMERITY
CAMPHOR	MUTTON	TETHERED
COLOSSAL	PALLID	TRUNCATED
CUPOLAS	PEPTONE	TUMULT
DECADENT	PHANTASM	VERDIGRIS
EDDYING	PRECOCIOUS	WAN
EKING	RECEDED	WHIM

Time Machine Vocabulary Word Search 4

```
C O L O S S A L A R T C E P S Z Y N D X
O U T E T H E R E D N E C R Q Z A M Y V
M B P T D E O G S B A K M A S W Q A L S
P M V O D E C A D E N T N E L U C C U S
E Q E U L P X M L S G N E A R A M E T W
N V L N G A E E S M I E D N P I M E K W
S E O T D L S L N S O L D E R V T I E S
A C C K O L D I O I P O Y C E E V Y T K
T A I B C I W O I N D D I D C R F F S Y
I M T H D D V R T O E N O E H X L L
O P Y B E J E A A R C I G T S I C D A R
N H Q P D C B T N H S G M E S G I E C L
S O X X E Z L I I C E Z U S I R N T K F
A R P D P U C N M A U F T A O I T A E X
U C E R M V E G O N Q W T I N S I C N D
R D P U I R K M B A I Z O C A C M N E V
I N T E R M I N A B L E N A L G A U D Y
A D O V J H N L T V E G Y C F F T R Y M
N S N G W S G S L Z D Y A A F B E T W M
S R E C O N D I T E Y R M L X Q M B B M
```

ABOMINATIONS	EKING	RECONDITE
ACACIAS	ELUDE	RILL
ALGAL	GAUDY	SAURIANS
AMELIORATING	IMPEDED	SHOAL
ANACHRONISMS	INDOLENT	SLACKENED
ANECDOTES	INTERMINABLE	SPECTRAL
BOLE	INTIMATE	SUCCULENT
CALAMITY	MACE	TEMERITY
CAMPHOR	MEEK	TETHERED
COLOSSAL	MUTTON	TRUNCATED
COMPENSATION	PALLID	TUMULT
CUPOLAS	PEPTONE	VELOCITY
DECADENT	POIGNANT	VERDIGRIS
DELIQUESCED	PRECESSIONAL	WAN
EDDYING	RECEDED	WHIM

Time Machine Vocabulary Word Search 4 Answer Key

```
C O L O S S A L A R T C E P S     N
O U T E T H E R E D N E C     A   M
M   P   E O         M   A W   M   A
P   V O D E C A D E N T N E L U C C U S
E   E U L   P   M L S G E E P A E E
N   L C   P   E E S I O A R I M E
S   O I   B   S L N S N N E V I   K
A   C T   D   I I N O P O C E Y   Y
T E A Y   E   O O R C D E R     S
I C M     D   R A N E O S D L
O   P     E   A T I R S T I     A
N H O     C   T N M N E E G   D C
S   R P   L   I   A C U S R I   K
A E D P U I R K   B A I       E N
U I   T     M I N A B L E G   T E
R N   O   W H   L           A G U D
I A       N G   L           T   R Y
A N                             E   R
N S   R E C O N D I T E         T
```

ABOMINATIONS	EKING	RECONDITE
ACACIAS	ELUDE	RILL
ALGAL	GAUDY	SAURIANS
AMELIORATING	IMPEDED	SHOAL
ANACHRONISMS	INDOLENT	SLACKENED
ANECDOTES	INTERMINABLE	SPECTRAL
BOLE	INTIMATE	SUCCULENT
CALAMITY	MACE	TEMERITY
CAMPHOR	MEEK	TETHERED
COLOSSAL	MUTTON	TRUNCATED
COMPENSATION	PALLID	TUMULT
CUPOLAS	PEPTONE	VELOCITY
DECADENT	POIGNANT	VERDIGRIS
DELIQUESCED	PRECESSIONAL	WAN
EDDYING	RECEDED	WHIM

Time Machine Vocabulary Crossword 1

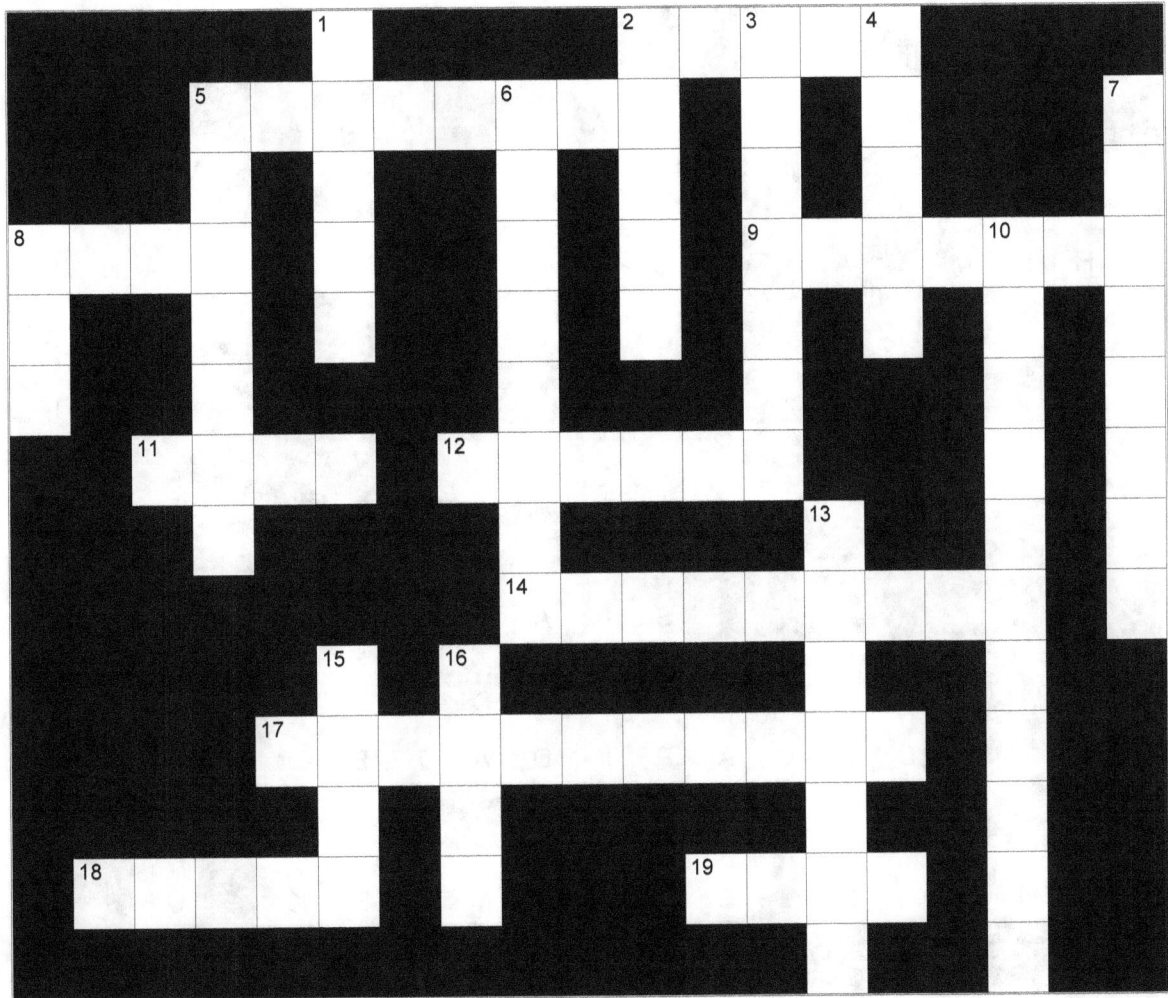

Across
2. Getting with great effort or strain
5. Huge
8. Odd or capricious notion or desire; a sudden fancy
9. Swirling as if in a whirlpool
11. Stem or trunk of a tree
12. Pale; faint or deficient in color
14. Made or became slower; slowed down
17. Fallen into partial ruin or decay, as from age, wear, or neglect
18. Sandbank or sand bar in a body of water exposed at low tide
19. Overly submissive or compliant; spiritless; tame

Down
1. Relating to algae
2. Avoid or escape by speed, cleverness or trickery
3. Slowed or obstructed the progress of
4. Brilliantly or excessively showy
5. Compound used in the manufacture of plastics and explosives
6. Lizards or similar reptiles
7. Dirty
8. Unnatural or sickly pallor; pallid; lacking color
10. Showing unbelief; skeptical
13. Moved away from; retreated; withdrew
15. Small brook; rivulet
16. Club-like, armor-breaking weapon of war

Time Machine Vocabulary Crossword 1 Answer Key

Across
2. Getting with great effort or strain
5. Huge
8. Odd or capricious notion or desire; a sudden fancy
9. Swirling as if in a whirlpool
11. Stem or trunk of a tree
12. Pale; faint or deficient in color
14. Made or became slower; slowed down
17. Fallen into partial ruin or decay, as from age, wear, or neglect
18. Sandbank or sand bar in a body of water exposed at low tide
19. Overly submissive or compliant; spiritless; tame

Down
1. Relating to algae
2. Avoid or escape by speed, cleverness or trickery
3. Slowed or obstructed the progress of
4. Brilliantly or excessively showy
5. Compound used in the manufacture of plastics and explosives
6. Lizards or similar reptiles
7. Dirty
8. Unnatural or sickly pallor; pallid; lacking color
10. Showing unbelief; skeptical
13. Moved away from; retreated; withdrew
15. Small brook; rivulet
16. Club-like, armor-breaking weapon of war

Time Machine Vocabulary Crossword 2

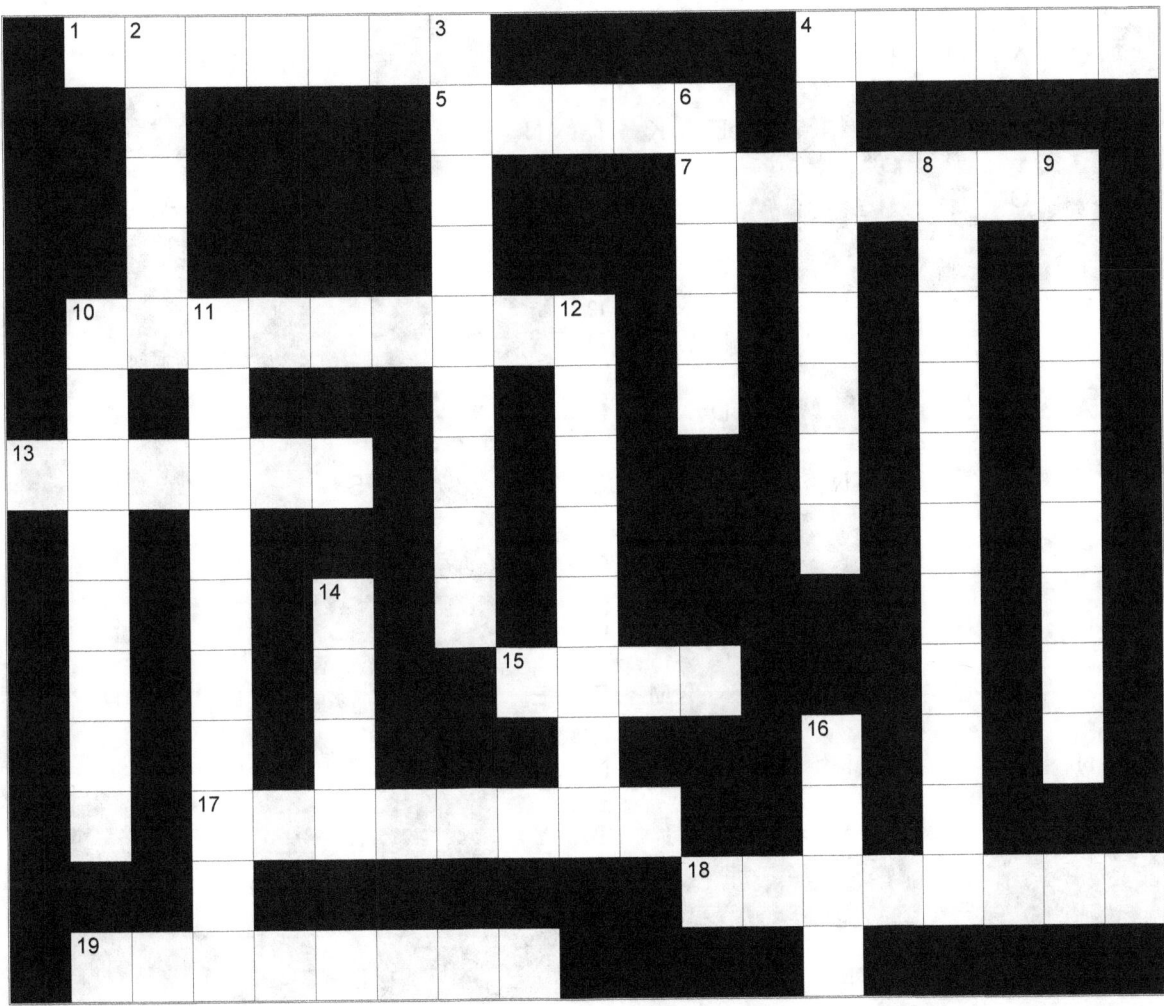

Across
1. Compound used in the manufacture of plastics and explosives
4. Pale; faint or deficient in color
5. Getting with great effort or strain
7. Fragrant yellow flowers used in perfumes
10. Made or became slower; slowed down
13. The meat of sheep
15. Overly submissive or compliant; spiritless; tame
17. Reckless boldness; rashness
18. Huge
19. Showing a disposition to avoid exertion; lazy

Down
2. Relating to algae
3. Dealing with very profound or difficult subject matter
4. Creation of the imagination or fancy; fantasy
6. Brilliantly or excessively showy
8. Showing unbelief; skeptical
9. Full of juice; juicy
10. Lizards or similar reptiles
11. Made thin
12. In a condition or process of mental or moral decay
14. Odd or capricious notion or desire; a sudden fancy
16. Stem or trunk of a tree

Time Machine Vocabulary Crossword 2 Answer Key

Across
1. Compound used in the manufacture of plastics and explosives
4. Pale; faint or deficient in color
5. Getting with great effort or strain
7. Fragrant yellow flowers used in perfumes
10. Made or became slower; slowed down
13. The meat of sheep
15. Overly submissive or compliant; spiritless; tame
17. Reckless boldness; rashness
18. Huge
19. Showing a disposition to avoid exertion; lazy

Down
2. Relating to algae
3. Dealing with very profound or difficult subject matter
4. Creation of the imagination or fancy; fantasy
6. Brilliantly or excessively showy
8. Showing unbelief; skeptical
9. Full of juice; juicy
10. Lizards or similar reptiles
11. Made thin
12. In a condition or process of mental or moral decay
14. Odd or capricious notion or desire; a sudden fancy
16. Stem or trunk of a tree

Time Machine Vocabulary Crossword 3

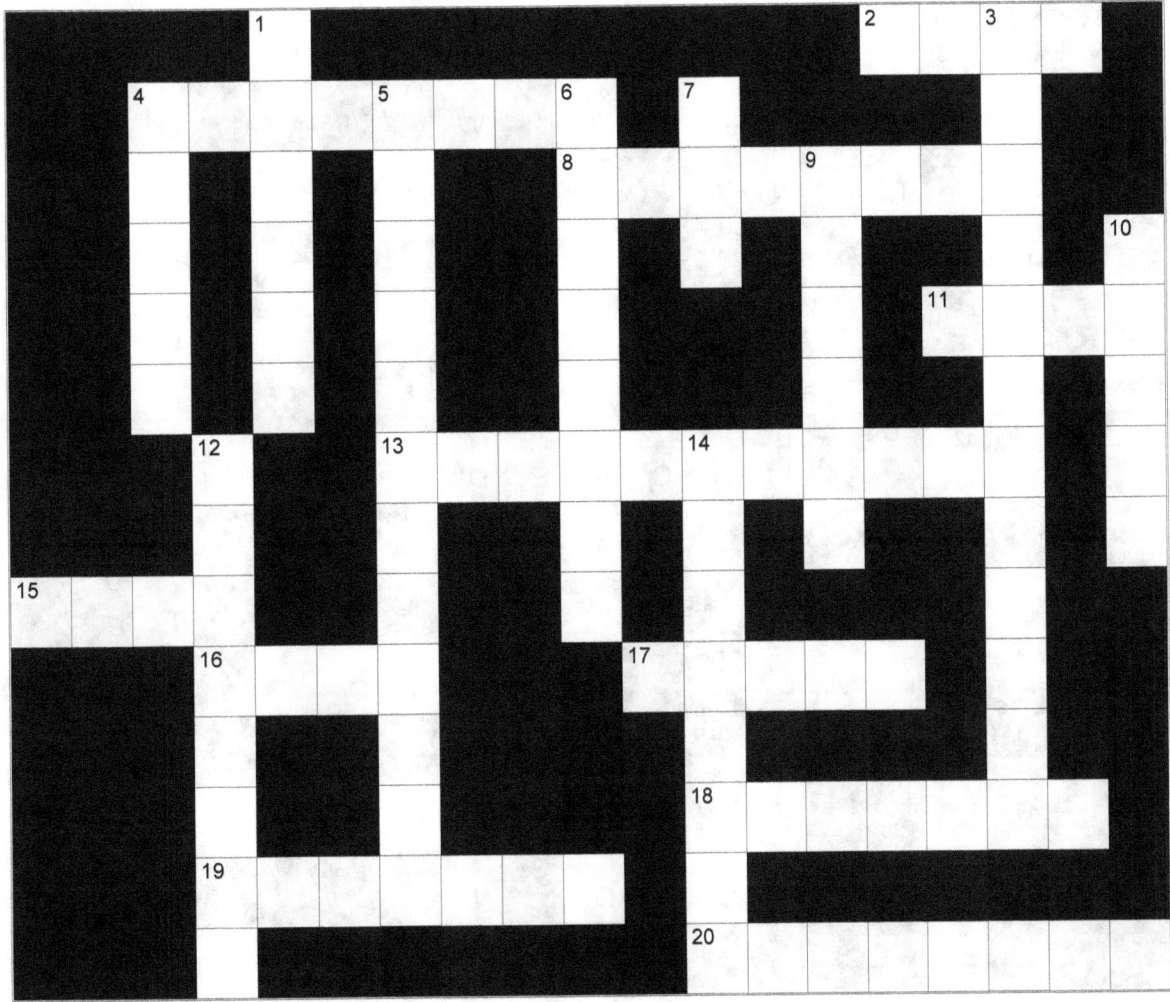

Across
2. Club-like, armor-breaking weapon of war
4. Lizards or similar reptiles
8. Creation of the imagination or fancy; fantasy
11. Overly submissive or compliant; spiritless; tame
13. Showing unbelief; skeptical
15. Stem or trunk of a tree
16. Small brook; rivulet
17. Brilliantly or excessively showy
18. Swirling as if in a whirlpool
19. Moved away from; retreated; withdrew
20. Reckless boldness; rashness

Down
1. The meat of sheep
3. Given or received in return for services or debt
4. Sandbank or sand bar in a body of water exposed at low tide
5. Lacking the ability to express oneself, esp. in clear speech
6. Ghostly
7. Unnatural or sickly pallor; pallid; lacking color
9. Highly distressing agitation of mind or feeling
10. Getting with great effort or strain
12. Opening, as a hole, slit, crack, or gap
14. In a condition or process of mental or moral decay

Time Machine Vocabulary Crossword 3 Answer Key

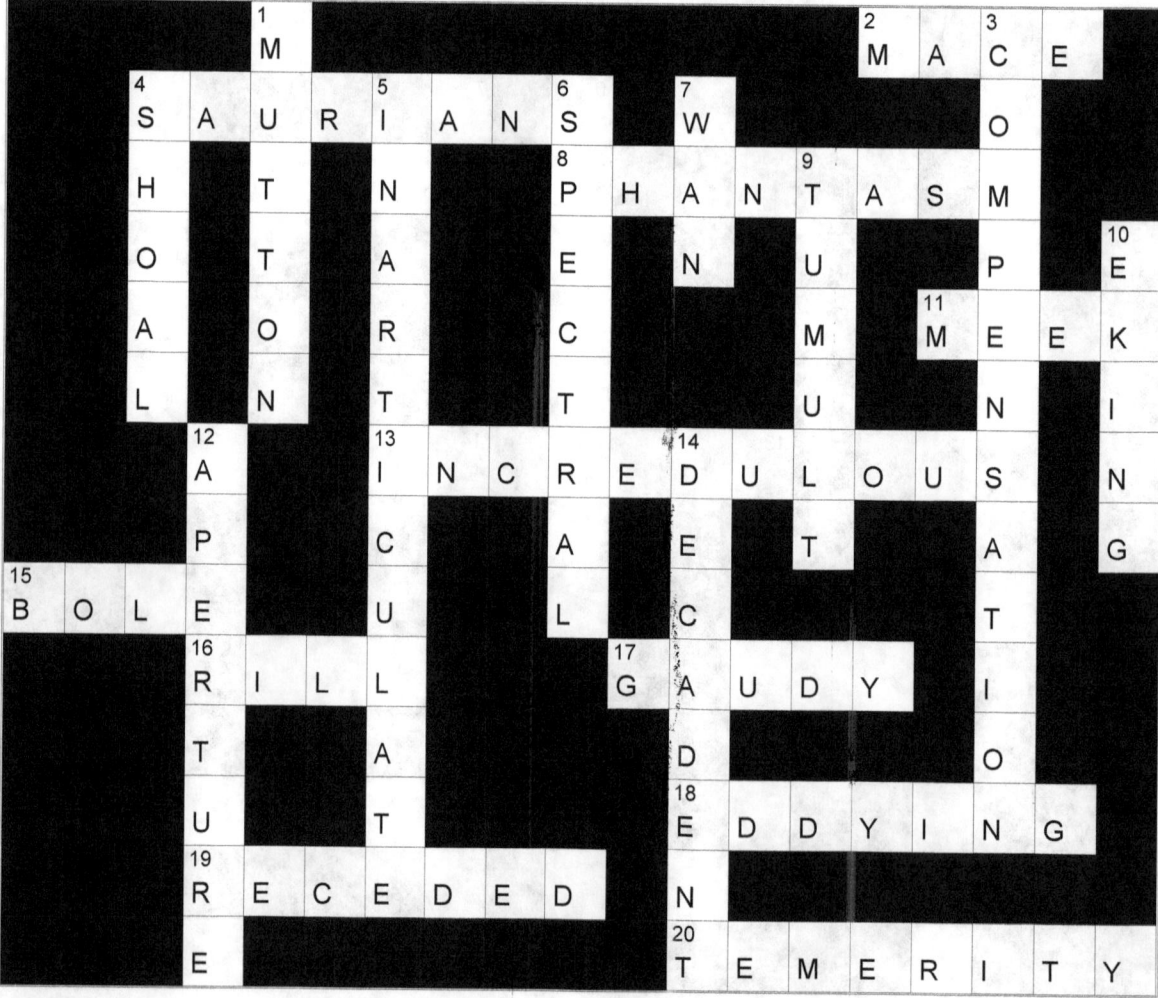

Across

2. Club-like, armor-breaking weapon of war
4. Lizards or similar reptiles
8. Creation of the imagination or fancy; fantasy
11. Overly submissive or compliant; spiritless; tame
13. Showing unbelief; skeptical
15. Stem or trunk of a tree
16. Small brook; rivulet
17. Brilliantly or excessively showy
18. Swirling as if in a whirlpool
19. Moved away from; retreated; withdrew
20. Reckless boldness; rashness

Down

1. The meat of sheep
3. Given or received in return for services or debt
4. Sandbank or sand bar in a body of water exposed at low tide
5. Lacking the ability to express oneself, esp. in clear speech
6. Ghostly
7. Unnatural or sickly pallor; pallid; lacking color
9. Highly distressing agitation of mind or feeling
10. Getting with great effort or strain
12. Opening, as a hole, slit, crack, or gap
14. In a condition or process of mental or moral decay

Time Machine Vocabulary Crossword 4

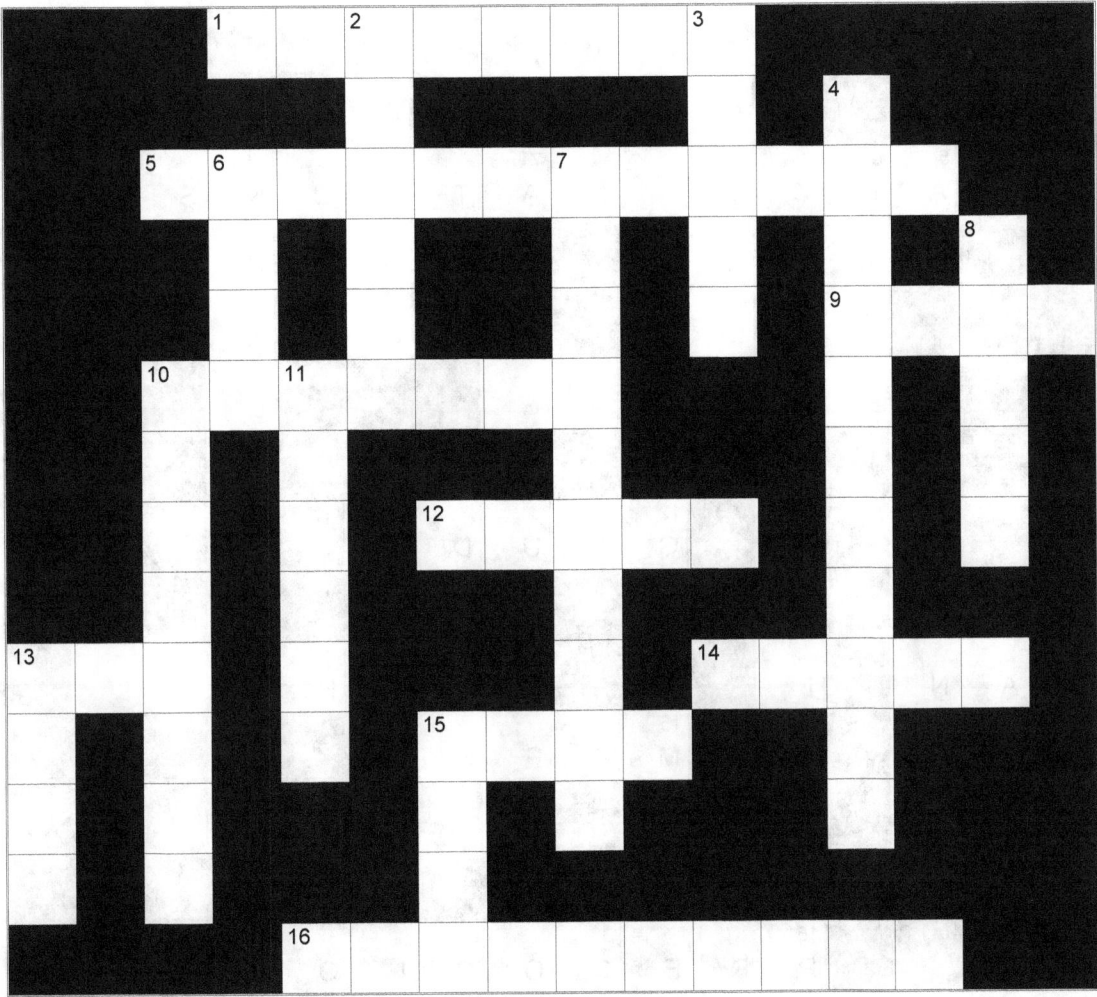

Across
1. To indicate or make known indirectly; hint; imply; suggest
5. Things that cause a sense of disgust
9. Small brook; rivulet
10. Complex water-soluble nutrient obtained by digesting protein
12. Brilliantly or excessively showy
13. Unnatural or sickly pallor; pallid; lacking color
14. Sandbank or sand bar in a body of water exposed at low tide
15. Overly submissive or compliant; spiritless; tame
16. Unusually advanced or mature in development, esp. mentally

Down
2. Highly distressing agitation of mind or feeling
3. Getting with great effort or strain
4. Showing unbelief; skeptical
6. Stem or trunk of a tree
7. Made thin
8. Relating to algae
10. Affecting or moving the emotions
11. Pale; faint or deficient in color
13. Odd or capricious notion or desire; a sudden fancy
15. Club-like, armor-breaking weapon of war

Time Machine Vocabulary Crossword 4 Answer Key

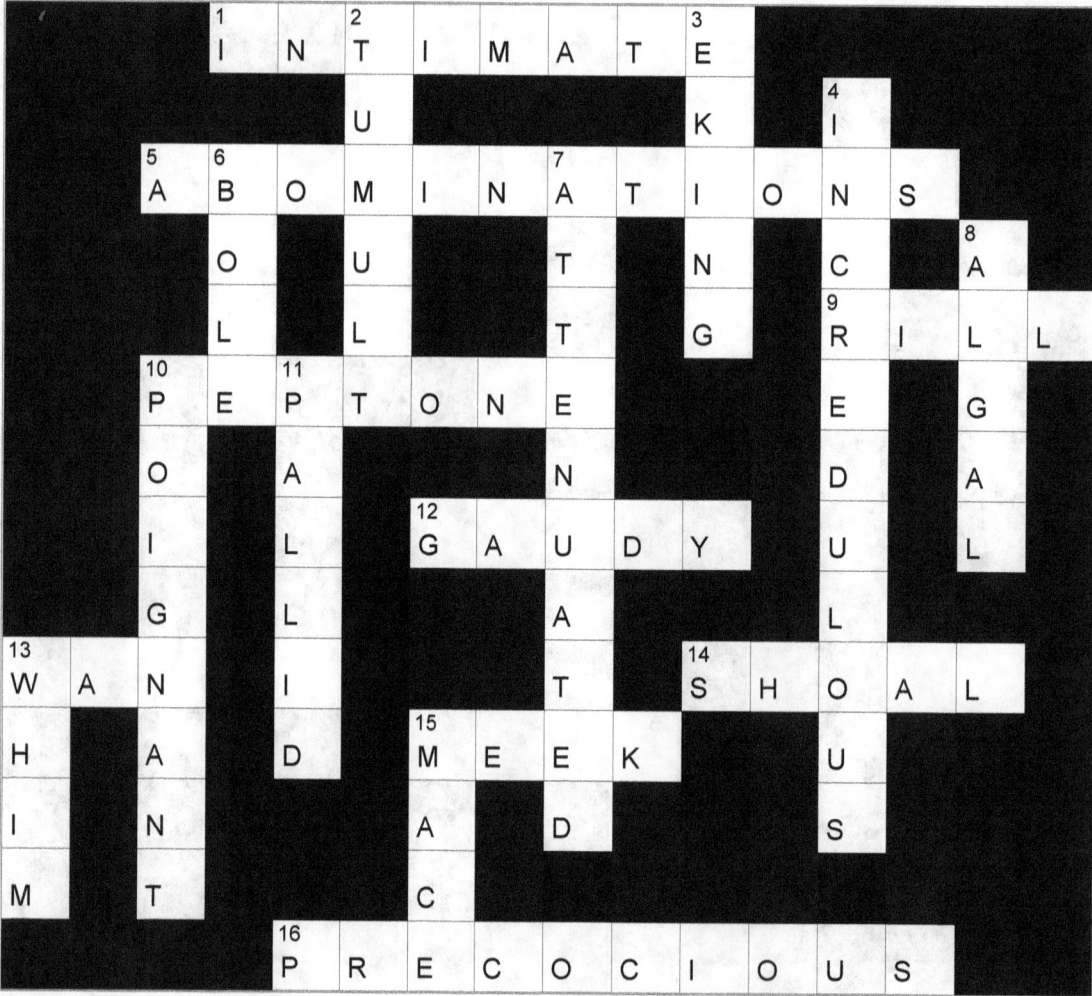

Across
1. To indicate or make known indirectly; hint; imply; suggest
5. Things that cause a sense of disgust
9. Small brook; rivulet
10. Complex water-soluble nutrient obtained by digesting protein
12. Brilliantly or excessively showy
13. Unnatural or sickly pallor; pallid; lacking color
14. Sandbank or sand bar in a body of water exposed at low tide
15. Overly submissive or compliant; spiritless; tame
16. Unusually advanced or mature in development, esp. mentally

Down
2. Highly distressing agitation of mind or feeling
3. Getting with great effort or strain
4. Showing unbelief; skeptical
6. Stem or trunk of a tree
7. Made thin
8. Relating to algae
10. Affecting or moving the emotions
11. Pale; faint or deficient in color
13. Odd or capricious notion or desire; a sudden fancy
15. Club-like, armor-breaking weapon of war

Time Machine Vocabulary Juggle Letters 1

1. TOLDENNI = 1. _____
   Showing a disposition to avoid exertion; lazy

2. OTAGNNPI = 2. _____
   Affecting or moving the emotions

3. ADKLEESCN = 3. _____
   Made or became slower; slowed down

4. ULNCUSETC = 4. _____
   Full of juice; juicy

5. ESDAOTNEC = 5. _____
   Short accounts of interesting or humorous incidents

6. LUTUMT = 6. _____
   Highly distressing agitation of mind or feeling

7. ECEDLUSQEDI = 7. _____
   Became liquid by absorbing moisture from the air

8. NOENICSAOMTP = 8. _____
   Given or received in return for services or debt

9. NNIBOOAMASTI = 9. _____
   Things that cause a sense of disgust

10. TEANEATDUT =10. _____
    Made thin

11. EUILSDUOCNR =11. _____
    Showing unbelief; skeptical

12. GIOIOSPUDR =12. _____
    Extraordinary in size, amount, extent, degree, force, etc.

13. REPUTARE =13. _____
    Opening, as a hole, slit, crack, or gap

14. DYEDGIN =14. _____
    Swirling as if in a whirlpool

15. UMTTON =15. _____
    The meat of sheep

Time Machine Vocabulary Juggle Letters 1 Answer Key

1. TOLDENNI = 1. INDOLENT
Showing a disposition to avoid exertion; lazy

2. OTAGNNPI = 2. POIGNANT
Affecting or moving the emotions

3. ADKLEESCN = 3. SLACKENED
Made or became slower; slowed down

4. ULNCUSETC = 4. SUCCULENT
Full of juice; juicy

5. ESDAOTNEC = 5. ANECDOTES
Short accounts of interesting or humorous incidents

6. LUTUMT = 6. TUMULT
Highly distressing agitation of mind or feeling

7. ECEDLUSQEDI = 7. DELIQUESCED
Became liquid by absorbing moisture from the air

8. NOENICSAOMTP = 8. COMPENSATION
Given or received in return for services or debt

9. NNIBOOAMASTI = 9. ABOMINATIONS
Things that cause a sense of disgust

10. TEANEATDUT = 10. ATTENUATED
Made thin

11. EUILSDUOCNR = 11. INCREDULOUS
Showing unbelief; skeptical

12. GIOIOSPUDR = 12. PRODIGIOUS
Extraordinary in size, amount, extent, degree, force, etc.

13. REPUTARE = 13. APERTURE
Opening, as a hole, slit, crack, or gap

14. DYEDGIN = 14. EDDYING
Swirling as if in a whirlpool

15. UMTTON = 15. MUTTON
The meat of sheep

Time Machine Vocabulary Juggle Letters 2

1. CSPAREIELONS = 1. _____
   Slow, conical motion of the earth's axis of rotation

2. TTLUUM = 2. _____
   Highly distressing agitation of mind or feeling

3. DIALLP = 3. _____
   Pale; faint or deficient in color

4. EEMK = 4. _____
   Overly submissive or compliant; spiritless; tame

5. DEEERCD = 5. _____
   Moved away from; retreated; withdrew

6. ICAMLTAY = 6. _____
   Great misfortune or disaster

7. ENDCATDE = 7. _____
   In a condition or process of mental or moral decay

8. LAGLA = 8. _____
   Relating to algae

9. ATILRNNEIMEB = 9. _____
   Unending

10. SUIGPDIROO =10. _____
    Extraordinary in size, amount, extent, degree, force, etc.

11. LQDCEEIUESD =11. _____
    Became liquid by absorbing moisture from the air

12. RTRUEAPE =12. _____
    Opening, as a hole, slit, crack, or gap

13. UYDAG =13. _____
    Brilliantly or excessively showy

14. TNPSMCAOEONI =14. _____
    Given or received in return for services or debt

Time Machine Vocabulary Juggle Letters 2 Answer Key

1. CSPAREIELONS = 1. PRECESSIONAL
   Slow, conical motion of the earth's axis of rotation

2. TTLUUM = 2. TUMULT
   Highly distressing agitation of mind or feeling

3. DIALLP = 3. PALLID
   Pale; faint or deficient in color

4. EEMK = 4. MEEK
   Overly submissive or compliant; spiritless; tame

5. DEEERCD = 5. RECEDED
   Moved away from; retreated; withdrew

6. ICAMLTAY = 6. CALAMITY
   Great misfortune or disaster

7. ENDCATDE = 7. DECADENT
   In a condition or process of mental or moral decay

8. LAGLA = 8. ALGAL
   Relating to algae

9. ATILRNNEIMEB = 9. INTERMINABLE
   Unending

10. SUIGPDIROO =10. PRODIGIOUS
    Extraordinary in size, amount, extent, degree, force, etc.

11. LQDCEEIUESD =11. DELIQUESCED
    Became liquid by absorbing moisture from the air

12. RTRUEAPE =12. APERTURE
    Opening, as a hole, slit, crack, or gap

13. UYDAG =13. GAUDY
    Brilliantly or excessively showy

14. TNPSMCAOEONI =14. COMPENSATION
    Given or received in return for services or debt

Time Machine Vocabulary Juggle Letters 3

1. IKEGN = 1. _____
Getting with great effort or strain

2. ITDEONLN = 2. _____
Showing a disposition to avoid exertion; lazy

3. RGROFUUSIOV = 3. _____
Feeding on fruit; fruit-eating

4. DOTICERNE = 4. _____
Dealing with very profound or difficult subject matter

5. ENAETDDC = 5. _____
In a condition or process of mental or moral decay

6. LIEVTYOC = 6. _____
Rapidity of motion or operation; swiftness; speed

7. ETAIITMN = 7. _____
To indicate or make known indirectly; hint; imply; suggest

8. EARUETRP = 8. _____
Opening, as a hole, slit, crack, or gap

9. MAYAITCL = 9. _____
Great misfortune or disaster

10. TUANTDEATE =10. _____
Made thin

11. DIEADLTPDAI =11. _____
Fallen into partial ruin or decay, as from age, wear, or neglect

12. EDTAURTNC =12. _____
Shortened by or as if by having a part cut off; cut short

13. INIOAABSTNMO =13. _____
Things that cause a sense of disgust

14. NUIAARSS =14. _____
Lizards or similar reptiles

Time Machine Vocabulary Juggle Letters 3 Answer Key

1. IKEGN = 1. EKING
   Getting with great effort or strain

2. ITDEONLN = 2. INDOLENT
   Showing a disposition to avoid exertion; lazy

3. RGROFUUSIOV = 3. FRUGIVOROUS
   Feeding on fruit; fruit-eating

4. DOTICERNE = 4. RECONDITE
   Dealing with very profound or difficult subject matter

5. ENAETDDC = 5. DECADENT
   In a condition or process of mental or moral decay

6. LIEVTYOC = 6. VELOCITY
   Rapidity of motion or operation; swiftness; speed

7. ETAIITMN = 7. INTIMATE
   To indicate or make known indirectly; hint; imply; suggest

8. EARUETRP = 8. APERTURE
   Opening, as a hole, slit, crack, or gap

9. MAYAITCL = 9. CALAMITY
   Great misfortune or disaster

10. TUANTDEATE =10. ATTENUATED
    Made thin

11. DIEADLTPDAI =11. DILAPIDATED
    Fallen into partial ruin or decay, as from age, wear, or neglect

12. EDTAURTNC =12. TRUNCATED
    Shortened by or as if by having a part cut off; cut short

13. INIOAABSTNMO =13. ABOMINATIONS
    Things that cause a sense of disgust

14. NUIAARSS =14. SAURIANS
    Lizards or similar reptiles

Time Machine Vocabulary Juggle Letters 4

1. IACCAAS = 1. _____
Fragrant yellow flowers used in perfumes

2. NUAEATTDET = 2. _____
Made thin

3. NLAIRETUICTA = 3. _____
Lacking the ability to express oneself, esp. in clear speech

4. TERRUAPE = 4. _____
Opening, as a hole, slit, crack, or gap

5. AIGNOPTN = 5. _____
Affecting or moving the emotions

6. ECSTULCUN = 6. _____
Full of juice; juicy

7. ANW = 7. _____
Unnatural or sickly pallor; pallid; lacking color

8. ITAIEMTN = 8. _____
To indicate or make known indirectly; hint; imply; suggest

9. LSOHA = 9. _____
Sandbank or sand bar in a body of water exposed at low tide

10. MRTYEITE = 10. _____
Reckless boldness; rashness

11. MALYATIC = 11. _____
Great misfortune or disaster

12. IVDRRIGSE = 12. _____
Blue-green crust formed on copper, brass, or bronze surfaces

13. CNDDTEEA = 13. _____
In a condition or process of mental or moral decay

14. DDEPMEI = 14. _____
Slowed or obstructed the progress of

Time Machine Vocabulary Juggle Letters 4 Answer Key

1. IACCAAS = 1. ACACIAS
   Fragrant yellow flowers used in perfumes

2. NUAEATTDET = 2. ATTENUATED
   Made thin

3. NLAIRETUICTA = 3. INARTICULATE
   Lacking the ability to express oneself, esp. in clear speech

4. TERRUAPE = 4. APERTURE
   Opening, as a hole, slit, crack, or gap

5. AIGNOPTN = 5. POIGNANT
   Affecting or moving the emotions

6. ECSTULCUN = 6. SUCCULENT
   Full of juice; juicy

7. ANW = 7. WAN
   Unnatural or sickly pallor; pallid; lacking color

8. ITAIEMTN = 8. INTIMATE
   To indicate or make known indirectly; hint; imply; suggest

9. LSOHA = 9. SHOAL
   Sandbank or sand bar in a body of water exposed at low tide

10. MRTYEITE = 10. TEMERITY
    Reckless boldness; rashness

11. MALYATIC = 11. CALAMITY
    Great misfortune or disaster

12. IVDRRIGSE = 12. VERDIGRIS
    Blue-green crust formed on copper, brass, or bronze surfaces

13. CNDDTEEA = 13. DECADENT
    In a condition or process of mental or moral decay

14. DDEPMEI = 14. IMPEDED
    Slowed or obstructed the progress of

ABOMINATIONS	Things that cause a sense of disgust
ACACIAS	Fragrant yellow flowers used in perfumes
ALGAL	Relating to algae
AMELIORATING	Making better, more bearable, or more satisfactory
ANACHRONISMS	Persons, objects, or practices that belong to a different time period
ANECDOTES	Short accounts of interesting or humorous incidents

APERTURE	Opening, as a hole, slit, crack, or gap
ATTENUATED	Made thin
BEGRIMED	Dirty
BOLE	Stem or trunk of a tree
CALAMITY	Great misfortune or disaster
CAMPHOR	Compound used in the manufacture of plastics and explosives

COLOSSAL	Huge
COMPENSATION	Given or received in return for services or debt
CONTRIVANCE	Device or control that is useful for a particular job
CUPOLAS	Small domes set on a round base or resting on pillars
DECADENT	In a condition or process of mental or moral decay
DELIQUESCED	Became liquid by absorbing moisture from the air

DILAPIDATED	Fallen into partial ruin or decay, as from age, wear, or neglect
EDDYING	Swirling as if in a whirlpool
EKING	Getting with great effort or strain
ELUDE	Avoid or escape by speed, cleverness or trickery
FRUGIVOROUS	Feeding on fruit; fruit-eating
GAUDY	Brilliantly or excessively showy

IMPARTIALITY	Showing no bias; neutrality
IMPEDED	Slowed or obstructed the progress of
INARTICULATE	Lacking the ability to express oneself, esp. in clear speech
INCREDULOUS	Showing unbelief; skeptical
INDOLENT	Showing a disposition to avoid exertion; lazy
INTERMINABLE	Unending

INTIMATE	To indicate or make known indirectly; hint; imply; suggest
MACE	Club-like, armor-breaking weapon of war
MEEK	Overly submissive or compliant; spiritless; tame
MUTTON	The meat of sheep
PALLID	Pale; faint or deficient in color
PEPTONE	Complex water-soluble nutrient obtained by digesting protein

PHANTASM	Creation of the imagination or fancy; fantasy
POIGNANT	Affecting or moving the emotions
PRECESSIONAL	Slow, conical motion of the earth's axis of rotation
PRECOCIOUS	Unusually advanced or mature in development, esp. mentally
PRETERNATURALLY	Out of the ordinary course of nature; exceptionally or abnormally
PRODIGIOUS	Extraordinary in size, amount, extent, degree, force, etc.

RECEDED	Moved away from; retreated; withdrew
RECONDITE	Dealing with very profound or difficult subject matter
RILL	Small brook; rivulet
SAURIANS	Lizards or similar reptiles
SHOAL	Sandbank or sand bar in a body of water exposed at low tide
SLACKENED	Made or became slower; slowed down

SPECTRAL	Ghostly
SUCCULENT	Full of juice; juicy
TEMERITY	Reckless boldness; rashness
TETHERED	Confined or restricted with or as if with a rope or chain
TRUNCATED	Shortened by or as if by having a part cut off; cut short
TUMULT	Highly distressing agitation of mind or feeling

VELOCITY	Rapidity of motion or operation; swiftness; speed
VERDIGRIS	Blue-green crust formed on copper, brass, or bronze surfaces
WAN	Unnatural or sickly pallor; pallid; lacking color
WHIM	Odd or capricious notion or desire; a sudden fancy

Time Machine Vocabulary

CALAMITY	COMPENSATION	PEPTONE	RECEDED	INTIMATE
PRECOCIOUS	INCREDULOUS	TETHERED	INARTICULATE	TUMULT
EKING	PRODIGIOUS	FREE SPACE	BEGRIMED	APERTURE
MEEK	SPECTRAL	EDDYING	PALLID	ACACIAS
TRUNCATED	IMPARTIALITY	POIGNANT	FRUGIVOROUS	DILAPIDATED

Time Machine Vocabulary

ANECDOTES	ELUDE	TEMERITY	DELIQUESCED	VELOCITY
AMELIORATING	WAN	RECONDITE	ALGAL	CONTRIVANCE
PHANTASM	BOLE	FREE SPACE	SHOAL	INTERMINABLE
INDOLENT	MACE	PRECESSIONAL	ANACHRONISMS	COLOSSAL
WHIM	IMPEDED	CAMPHOR	PRETER-NATURALLY	DECADENT

Time Machine Vocabulary

MEEK	WHIM	ACACIAS	INCREDULOUS	DILAPIDATED
FRUGIVOROUS	TETHERED	PRECESSIONAL	ALGAL	PRECOCIOUS
IMPEDED	APERTURE	FREE SPACE	INTERMINABLE	SUCCULENT
INDOLENT	EDDYING	TRUNCATED	RECEDED	COLOSSAL
SHOAL	CAMPHOR	IMPARTIALITY	VERDIGRIS	MACE

Time Machine Vocabulary

CONTRIVANCE	DELIQUESCED	INTIMATE	TUMULT	RECONDITE
EKING	POIGNANT	SLACKENED	SPECTRAL	PRODIGIOUS
INARTICULATE	DECADENT	FREE SPACE	TEMERITY	PHANTASM
PEPTONE	COMPENSATION	GAUDY	SAURIANS	ATTENUATED
ANACHRONISMS	WAN	CALAMITY	ELUDE	CUPOLAS

Time Machine Vocabulary

ANACHRONISMS	MUTTON	RECONDITE	ALGAL	TUMULT
CALAMITY	SLACKENED	PRECOCIOUS	MACE	WHIM
BOLE	ATTENUATED	FREE SPACE	GAUDY	AMELIORATING
TEMERITY	SPECTRAL	COLOSSAL	COMPENSATION	WAN
INTERMINABLE	PALLID	EDDYING	INCREDULOUS	CAMPHOR

Time Machine Vocabulary

VERDIGRIS	DELIQUESCED	BEGRIMED	TRUNCATED	INARTICULATE
ANECDOTES	SAURIANS	RECEDED	IMPEDED	INDOLENT
IMPARTIALITY	SHOAL	FREE SPACE	VELOCITY	INTIMATE
MEEK	ELUDE	PEPTONE	FRUGIVOROUS	TETHERED
PRODIGIOUS	APERTURE	POIGNANT	RILL	DILAPIDATED

Time Machine Vocabulary

IMPARTIALITY	TETHERED	ANECDOTES	IMPEDED	EKING
PRODIGIOUS	SHOAL	MUTTON	COMPENSATION	MACE
SPECTRAL	RECEDED	FREE SPACE	ELUDE	MEEK
INDOLENT	CUPOLAS	TEMERITY	ACACIAS	VELOCITY
SUCCULENT	TRUNCATED	ANACHRONISMS	ABOMINATIONS	WAN

Time Machine Vocabulary

FRUGIVOROUS	GAUDY	PHANTASM	SAURIANS	WHIM
INTIMATE	RILL	COLOSSAL	RECONDITE	VERDIGRIS
ALGAL	AMELIORATING	FREE SPACE	INARTICULATE	ATTENUATED
CALAMITY	SLACKENED	EDDYING	PALLID	POIGNANT
PRETER-NATURALLY	INTERMINABLE	CONTRIVANCE	DELIQUESCED	PRECESSIONAL

Time Machine Vocabulary

PHANTASM	POIGNANT	ANACHRONISMS	ACACIAS	ANECDOTES
RECONDITE	PRETER-NATURALLY	MEEK	FRUGIVOROUS	DELIQUESCED
BEGRIMED	SLACKENED	FREE SPACE	CUPOLAS	PRODIGIOUS
COMPENSATION	MACE	EDDYING	VERDIGRIS	RILL
WAN	WHIM	APERTURE	SUCCULENT	TUMULT

Time Machine Vocabulary

PRECESSIONAL	AMELIORATING	GAUDY	COLOSSAL	SHOAL
MUTTON	BOLE	SAURIANS	INTIMATE	DILAPIDATED
INDOLENT	ALGAL	FREE SPACE	ELUDE	DECADENT
PALLID	VELOCITY	INCREDULOUS	ABOMINATIONS	INTERMINABLE
TETHERED	EKING	SPECTRAL	PRECOCIOUS	IMPARTIALITY

Time Machine Vocabulary

INARTICULATE	IMPEDED	IMPARTIALITY	VERDIGRIS	MACE
CUPOLAS	ACACIAS	INCREDULOUS	ANECDOTES	RECEDED
DECADENT	SHOAL	FREE SPACE	EDDYING	PRECOCIOUS
SLACKENED	SAURIANS	RILL	WHIM	COLOSSAL
ANACHRONISMS	DELIQUESCED	GAUDY	PRETER-NATURALLY	INTERMINABLE

Time Machine Vocabulary

RECONDITE	ELUDE	ATTENUATED	ALGAL	DILAPIDATED
TUMULT	BOLE	FRUGIVOROUS	PHANTASM	CAMPHOR
POIGNANT	PRECESSIONAL	FREE SPACE	APERTURE	TETHERED
INDOLENT	AMELIORATING	PRODIGIOUS	SPECTRAL	WAN
PALLID	EKING	CONTRIVANCE	TEMERITY	ABOMINATIONS

Time Machine Vocabulary

APERTURE	SPECTRAL	ELUDE	TETHERED	ABOMINATIONS
EKING	INDOLENT	PALLID	INTIMATE	SLACKENED
DECADENT	RECEDED	FREE SPACE	VELOCITY	CALAMITY
TRUNCATED	SAURIANS	WAN	AMELIORATING	SUCCULENT
DELIQUESCED	GAUDY	COLOSSAL	ALGAL	IMPEDED

Time Machine Vocabulary

PRECOCIOUS	PHANTASM	MACE	INARTICULATE	INTERMINABLE
MUTTON	BOLE	POIGNANT	PRECESSIONAL	WHIM
BEGRIMED	DILAPIDATED	FREE SPACE	FRUGIVOROUS	MEEK
VERDIGRIS	ACACIAS	ANACHRONISMS	RECONDITE	PRETER-NATURALLY
EDDYING	INCREDULOUS	PRODIGIOUS	ATTENUATED	CAMPHOR

Time Machine Vocabulary

WAN	MUTTON	BEGRIMED	ANACHRONISMS	MEEK
SUCCULENT	ATTENUATED	BOLE	ANECDOTES	PRETER-NATURALLY
ALGAL	INDOLENT	FREE SPACE	COMPENSATION	PHANTASM
APERTURE	EKING	PRODIGIOUS	ABOMINATIONS	RECEDED
DELIQUESCED	PRECESSIONAL	POIGNANT	FRUGIVOROUS	PRECOCIOUS

Time Machine Vocabulary

GAUDY	CONTRIVANCE	SHOAL	TETHERED	WHIM
EDDYING	DECADENT	CUPOLAS	RILL	VELOCITY
RECONDITE	PEPTONE	FREE SPACE	PALLID	CAMPHOR
SAURIANS	IMPARTIALITY	VERDIGRIS	TEMERITY	DILAPIDATED
SLACKENED	INARTICULATE	INTIMATE	ELUDE	IMPEDED

Time Machine Vocabulary

AMELIORATING	SPECTRAL	INCREDULOUS	CONTRIVANCE	INDOLENT
SAURIANS	TRUNCATED	SHOAL	PALLID	ACACIAS
SLACKENED	TEMERITY	FREE SPACE	TUMULT	IMPARTIALITY
IMPEDED	ATTENUATED	ELUDE	PEPTONE	DELIQUESCED
CAMPHOR	ABOMINATIONS	RECEDED	PHANTASM	ANECDOTES

Time Machine Vocabulary

MEEK	INTERMINABLE	SUCCULENT	BOLE	EKING
DECADENT	VELOCITY	FRUGIVOROUS	TETHERED	PRECOCIOUS
APERTURE	EDDYING	FREE SPACE	COMPENSATION	CALAMITY
WAN	BEGRIMED	CUPOLAS	INARTICULATE	ANACHRONISMS
GAUDY	PRODIGIOUS	COLOSSAL	WHIM	INTIMATE

Time Machine Vocabulary

BOLE	ANACHRONISMS	SUCCULENT	PRECOCIOUS	DILAPIDATED
ACACIAS	AMELIORATING	WAN	TEMERITY	IMPARTIALITY
EKING	TETHERED	FREE SPACE	IMPEDED	ALGAL
MACE	PALLID	INARTICULATE	PRECESSIONAL	RECEDED
SLACKENED	INCREDULOUS	POIGNANT	MEEK	DELIQUESCED

Time Machine Vocabulary

SPECTRAL	PEPTONE	CUPOLAS	VELOCITY	SAURIANS
ATTENUATED	INDOLENT	VERDIGRIS	FRUGIVOROUS	ABOMINATIONS
BEGRIMED	COMPENSATION	FREE SPACE	CALAMITY	PRETER-NATURALLY
ELUDE	DECADENT	COLOSSAL	SHOAL	INTIMATE
CAMPHOR	EDDYING	TUMULT	RECONDITE	APERTURE

Time Machine Vocabulary

SAURIANS	FRUGIVOROUS	RILL	APERTURE	SPECTRAL
TRUNCATED	EKING	TETHERED	RECEDED	EDDYING
COLOSSAL	MACE	FREE SPACE	INTIMATE	CALAMITY
SLACKENED	TUMULT	TEMERITY	PRETER-NATURALLY	ANECDOTES
MEEK	PALLID	CUPOLAS	INDOLENT	PRECESSIONAL

Time Machine Vocabulary

PRODIGIOUS	WHIM	SHOAL	DILAPIDATED	ELUDE
ABOMINATIONS	GAUDY	ALGAL	PHANTASM	COMPENSATION
BOLE	SUCCULENT	FREE SPACE	CONTRIVANCE	VELOCITY
DELIQUESCED	PRECOCIOUS	PEPTONE	INTERMINABLE	IMPARTIALITY
VERDIGRIS	IMPEDED	ACACIAS	INCREDULOUS	INARTICULATE

Time Machine Vocabulary

CONTRIVANCE	CUPOLAS	ANACHRONISMS	FRUGIVOROUS	PRODIGIOUS
POIGNANT	WAN	ATTENUATED	GAUDY	VELOCITY
INDOLENT	APERTURE	FREE SPACE	IMPEDED	COMPENSATION
RECEDED	TEMERITY	COLOSSAL	TRUNCATED	MUTTON
SUCCULENT	PALLID	INARTICULATE	PHANTASM	ELUDE

Time Machine Vocabulary

BOLE	SAURIANS	AMELIORATING	SPECTRAL	ACACIAS
MEEK	ANECDOTES	INCREDULOUS	SHOAL	CALAMITY
DECADENT	RILL	FREE SPACE	PRECOCIOUS	EDDYING
TUMULT	WHIM	EKING	BEGRIMED	PRECESSIONAL
PRETER-NATURALLY	IMPARTIALITY	CAMPHOR	SLACKENED	ABOMINATIONS

Time Machine Vocabulary

ELUDE	SHOAL	MUTTON	INCREDULOUS	CAMPHOR
PRETER-NATURALLY	ABOMINATIONS	SAURIANS	FRUGIVOROUS	IMPEDED
COLOSSAL	INDOLENT	FREE SPACE	EDDYING	WAN
TRUNCATED	SUCCULENT	RECONDITE	INARTICULATE	MEEK
DILAPIDATED	BEGRIMED	TEMERITY	EKING	ALGAL

Time Machine Vocabulary

PALLID	SLACKENED	ATTENUATED	WHIM	BOLE
INTERMINABLE	DELIQUESCED	ANACHRONISMS	INTIMATE	TETHERED
CALAMITY	RECEDED	FREE SPACE	DECADENT	PRECOCIOUS
CUPOLAS	IMPARTIALITY	ANECDOTES	TUMULT	CONTRIVANCE
GAUDY	PHANTASM	PRODIGIOUS	MACE	COMPENSATION

Time Machine Vocabulary

ALGAL	DELIQUESCED	PALLID	VERDIGRIS	DILAPIDATED
TEMERITY	CONTRIVANCE	EDDYING	PRECOCIOUS	WHIM
PRETER-NATURALLY	RECONDITE	FREE SPACE	GAUDY	SAURIANS
INTERMINABLE	BEGRIMED	RILL	APERTURE	PEPTONE
IMPEDED	ELUDE	MUTTON	MEEK	CUPOLAS

Time Machine Vocabulary

SLACKENED	COMPENSATION	WAN	MACE	SPECTRAL
VELOCITY	TETHERED	ATTENUATED	TUMULT	COLOSSAL
DECADENT	PRECESSIONAL	FREE SPACE	BOLE	POIGNANT
CALAMITY	ABOMINATIONS	AMELIORATING	IMPARTIALITY	SHOAL
ANECDOTES	INDOLENT	RECEDED	INTIMATE	FRUGIVOROUS

Time Machine Vocabulary

COLOSSAL	IMPARTIALITY	INTIMATE	ATTENUATED	CUPOLAS
SAURIANS	GAUDY	MACE	RECONDITE	DILAPIDATED
COMPENSATION	FRUGIVOROUS	FREE SPACE	AMELIORATING	TEMERITY
RECEDED	ANECDOTES	SHOAL	VELOCITY	CONTRIVANCE
INTERMINABLE	EKING	BEGRIMED	APERTURE	DECADENT

Time Machine Vocabulary

BOLE	IMPEDED	TRUNCATED	ALGAL	ACACIAS
INCREDULOUS	PALLID	CALAMITY	CAMPHOR	POIGNANT
RILL	PEPTONE	FREE SPACE	INDOLENT	INARTICULATE
DELIQUESCED	SUCCULENT	ABOMINATIONS	MEEK	VERDIGRIS
SPECTRAL	PRETER-NATURALLY	TUMULT	EDDYING	PRECESSIONAL

Time Machine Vocabulary

CONTRIVANCE	POIGNANT	INDOLENT	VELOCITY	ATTENUATED
EKING	CAMPHOR	ACACIAS	ANECDOTES	MACE
APERTURE	WAN	FREE SPACE	BOLE	SHOAL
PRECOCIOUS	INCREDULOUS	MUTTON	PEPTONE	EDDYING
PHANTASM	DECADENT	TRUNCATED	DILAPIDATED	SAURIANS

Time Machine Vocabulary

COLOSSAL	ABOMINATIONS	INTERMINABLE	TETHERED	COMPENSATION
PRECESSIONAL	PRODIGIOUS	TUMULT	INTIMATE	GAUDY
RILL	SLACKENED	FREE SPACE	WHIM	BEGRIMED
AMELIORATING	SUCCULENT	DELIQUESCED	ALGAL	CALAMITY
CUPOLAS	INARTICULATE	IMPARTIALITY	MEEK	ANACHRONISMS